Editor-in-Chief and Founder:
   Lyndon H. LaRouche, Jr.
Editorial Board: *Lyndon H. LaRouche, Jr. , Helga
   Zepp-LaRouche, Robert Ingraham, Tony
   Papert, Gerald Rose, Dennis Small, Jeffrey
   Steinberg, William Wertz*
Co-Editors: *Robert Ingraham, Tony Papert*
Technology: *Marsha Freeman*
Transcriptions: *Katherine Notley*
Ebooks: *Richard Burden*
Graphics: *Alan Yue*
Photos: *Stuart Lewis*
Circulation Manager: *Stanley Ezrol*

INTELLIGENCE DIRECTORS
Economics: *Marcia Merry Baker, Paul Gallagher*
History: *Anton Chaitkin*
Ibero-America: *Dennis Small*
Russia and Eastern Europe: *Rachel Douglas*
United States: *Debra Freeman*

INTERNATIONAL BUREAUS
Bogotá: *Miriam Redondo*
Berlin: *Rainer Apel*
Copenhagen: *Tom Gillesberg*
Lima: *Sara Madueño*
Melbourne: *Robert Barwick*
Mexico City: *Gerardo Castilleja Chávez*
New Delhi: *Ramtanu Maitra*
Paris: *Christine Bierre*
Stockholm: *Ulf Sandmark*
United Nations, N.Y.C.: *Leni Rubinstein*
Washington, D.C.: *William Jones*
Wiesbaden: *Göran Haglund*

ON THE WEB
e-mail: eirns@larouchepub.com
www.larouchepub.com
www.executiveintelligencereview.com
www.larouchepub.com/eiw
Webmaster: *John Sigerson*
Assistant Webmaster: *George Hollis*
Editor, Arabic-language edition: *Hussein Askary*

EIR (ISSN 0273-6314) *is published weekly
(50 issues), by EIR News Service, Inc.,
P.O. Box 17390, Washington, D.C. 20041-0390.
(703) 297-8434*

European Headquarters: E.I.R. GmbH, Postfach
Bahnstrasse 9a, D-65205, Wiesbaden, Germany
Tel: 49-611-73650
Homepage: http://www.eir.de
e-mail: info@eir.de
Director: Georg Neudecker

Montreal, Canada: 514-461-1557
eir@eircanada.ca

Denmark: EIR - Danmark, Sankt Knuds Vej 11,
basement left, DK-1903 Frederiksberg, Denmark.
Tel.: +45 35 43 60 40, Fax: +45 35 43 87 57. e-mail:
eirdk@hotmail.com.

Mexico City: EIR, Sor Juana Inés de la Cruz 242-2
Col. Agricultura C.P. 11360
Delegación M. Hidalgo, México D.F.
Tel. (5525) 5318-2301
eirmexico@gmail.com

Copyright: ©2018 EIR News Service. All rights
reserved. Reproduction in whole or in part without
permission strictly prohibited.

Canada Post Publication Sales Agreement
#40683579

Postmaster: Send all address changes to *EIR*, P.O.
Box 17390, Washington, D.C. 20041-0390.

Signed articles in *EIR* represent the views of the authors,
and not necessarily those of the Editorial Board.

Two World Systems

EIRContents

www.larouchepub.com   Volume 45, Number 26, June 29, 2018

ZEPP-LAROUCHE WEBCAST

Change for the Better Is Coming, If You Fight for It

This is the edited transcript of the June 21, 2018 Schiller Institute New Paradigm webcast, an interview with the founder of the Schiller Institutes, Helga Zepp-LaRouche. She was interviewed by Harley Schlanger. A video *of the webcast is available.*

Harley Schlanger: Hello, I'm Harley Schlanger with the Schiller Institute. Welcome to our webcast this week, featuring our founder, Helga Zepp-LaRouche.

Since our program last week, Helga has drafted a memo that is being circulated widely in government circles and to institutions such as the United Nations, and at events and forums. It should be circulated everywhere. It's titled "Follow the Example of Singapore!" This really shapes what we want to start with today. What Helga described is the process that was unleashed, leading into the meeting between President Trump and North Korea's Chairman Kim Jong-un and its stunning outcome.

So Helga, why don't we start with the memo that you drafted?

Helga Zepp-LaRouche: President Trump and Chairman Kim Jong-un were able to completely transform a very dangerous situation around North Korea within a few months, into the total opposite: from being the potential trigger point of World War III, to being, instead, a hopeful perspective. North Korea can now be integrated into the Belt and Road Initiative, with the support of the United States, China and Russia. The promise of security guarantees, eventually lifting sanctions, and complete denuclearization are part of integrating North Korea

with the Belt and Road Initiative. If this works, as it promises to, making North Korea a prosperous country, this will be a really groundbreaking set of developments. As President Trump said at his press conference, "The past does not have to define our future."

That is obviously proof that you can turn the worst situation around if you have an inspiration, a vision,

Irish Naval personnel rescuing migrants, June 15, 2015, as part of the EU's Mediterranean border patrol.

and the political will to carry it out.

We now have a series of complete destabilizations in the West. The refugee crisis is threatening to completely rip apart the so-called European unity, which is actually nonexistent; it could end the chancellorship of Angela Merkel within less than two weeks. The border crisis between the United States and Mexico also shows that the immigrant question is out of control and needs to be addressed.

The Singapore Model

The proposals by the European Union and by different factions of the German government, are all completely unworkable. These plans are brutal and barbaric—creating camps outside the borders of the European Union in North African countries, to warehouse refugees and deter them from coming to Europe—this is barbaric. All the people who were so freaked out about Trump ripping the babies from the breasts of their mothers— these are the same people and the same media who have no problem in proposing camps in countries that have no clear government control. There are many reports that people in these camps have been sold into slavery, have been raped and tortured. They are subject to absolutely terrible conditions. But, if the real root causes of why people are coming to Europe are not addressed—the horrible conditions in many parts of Africa, where people face impossible situations, then there will never be a workable solution.

I have proposed in this memorandum, which Harley just mentioned, that the EU follow the example of Singapore. The EU should change the agenda of their upcoming summit, which will take place in a week, and instead put only one issue on the agenda: The real development of Africa. Invite President Xi Jinping because he has enormous credibility in Africa. The Chinese government has led investment in railways and industrial parks, in hydropower and many, many projects. The EU should invite some of the African heads of state who have already achieved great results by cooperating with China in these projects.

If the European leaders—plus Xi Jinping and half a

Xinhua/Li Baishun

Xinhua/Chen Yaqin

Chinese projects in Africa. Above, the Soubre hydroelectric power station built by China in Ivory Coast. Below, China's Sinohydro expanded the production of electricity on the Zimbabwe side of the Kariba Dam, to produce an additional 300 MW for the Zimbabwe grid.

dozen African leaders who would speak for the continent—would declare a crash program for the infrastructure development of Africa, not only would such an action have credibility, because of Xi Jinping's presence, but it would signal to all relevant governments and all young people, that there exists a great opportunity to cooperate in the construction of their own countries. Many, many people would no longer feel compelled to traverse the Sahara, risking death by thirst, or death by drowning in the Mediterranean, or risk being captured by Frontex (the EU border police) to then be herded into what even the Pope has characterized as "concentration camps."

I think this positive agenda can be made to happen. Now, it's not so likely, however, that the EU will be the institution that does this, given the fact that they are what they are, but this is absolutely the correct idea, and if this EU summit misses this opportunity, then one can have a summit at any time, in July or August, or one can even use the UN General Assembly in September to make that issue the only point on the agenda.

The same can be applied to the United States. President Trump should have a summit with Xi Jinping and with leaders of Ibero-America, and there, do the same thing: commit to joint ventures between the United States, China and Latin American countries, to transform the continent and eliminate the poverty, which is the reason why people are now flooding into the United States.

I think this approach is eminently feasible. It is the only way to solve the problem. I'm very happy that my call has found good responses. It has been translated into eight languages already, including the most important European languages, Chinese, Russian, Japanese, and Korean. I would ask all of you who are watching this program to help us circulate this call, and also the call issued by Kesha Rogers, the Texas congressional candidate who is focusing on the American aspect. Please help us circulate these calls. Get onboard this mobilization because it is extremely urgent that this approach be taken now.

Schlanger: I think it's most important that your proposal breaks the controlled debate. The reason that we're in this mess today is that the debate has been phony: Either let the borders be opened and let nations be overrun, or clamp down the borders. Missing from the discussion, as you say, are the generating processes that have been wars and poverty.

In the last few weeks, since the Singapore summit, Trump has been moving toward going ahead with a summit with President Putin of Russia, which again, breaks the controlled environment. Do you think such a summit would contribute positively to resolving the forced migration crisis? Would you give Trump the advice that he should take up your proposal in his meeting with Putin?

Zepp-LaRouche: I think that a meeting between Putin and Trump is the next important item on the strategic agenda. Active preparations are now being made for such a meeting, possibly taking place in July, possibly in Vienna. I think this is now possible with Russiagate falling apart. U.S. Department of Justice Inspector General Michael Horowitz testified to a Senate hearing—remember his investigation and report was only on the email scandal around Hillary Clinton—that there was unprecedented bias on the part of all of the people involved in the Clinton investigation, and that Trump was completely justified in firing FBI Director James Comey. I think this has freed Trump to move forward on this front.

Dangers of Trade War

Let me raise another issue, because there are unfortunate escalations in possible trade war. Trump raised the possibility of imposing tariffs on $450 billion in imports from China, and there are now countermeasures going into effect. Tomorrow the EU will put in countermeasures. Turkey, Canada and Mexico are also putting up new tariffs, and there is a great danger of an ever escalating trade war.

The Chinese are very indignant, saying this is completely counterproductive; this is a lose-lose policy. Many people who voted for Trump—farmers and industrialists—are now being hurt by these tariffs and are in danger of going bankrupt. This is no good.

I have proposed the Singapore approach as a solution. Were the United States and China to engage in joint ventures to develop the countries of Central and South America, trade volume would increase significantly, in a multilateral way. The trade imbalances would be overcome through increased trade. I would like to get this message out, in particular, to the Trump voters who are affected by these policies—farmers, people and companies that have investments both in China and in the United States, all of whom are now in danger of going bankrupt, putting many jobs at risk. I ask our listeners to move on our "Singapore solution" proposal and to get the message to President Trump. We have to counter the ideologues in the Trump camp who are so anti-China and who are such extreme neo-liberal free-traders that they are giving him advice that could potentially turn his base away from him.

Trump, while continuing to having his excellent relationship with Xi Jinping, can add to that an excellent relationship with Putin. He can expand on the direction he so courageously accomplished in Singapore with North Korea. He can take the same approach—the predicates are different, but the approach would be the same—turn a bad policy, a lose-lose policy, into the opposite: go with win-win cooperation. The world is urgently in need of such a policy change. I think it can be done! The fact that the Singapore summit took place, is the proof that you can completely change a policy when it is leading nowhere.

The West right now is faced with the decision: either change policy, or collapse. That is what is at stake. So I appeal to all Trump supporters; pick up on this proposal and help us turn this around.

Schlanger: On this matter of being able to change

Japan's Prime Minister Shinzo Abe (right front) meets China's State Councilor and Foreign Minister Wang Yi in Tokyo, Japan, April 16, 2018.

relations from the past to a completely new relationship, we've seen that starting to take place between India and China, with the Modi meeting with Xi Jinping. There are also some significant developments that just took place between Japan and China.

Zepp-LaRouche: Yes, this is very good. In recent history, there had been deep mistrust between China and Japan. The history between those two countries during the period of World War II left deep scars. But, this is all now past, starting a year ago last May, when Prime Minister Shinzo Abe sent his number two, the head of the Liberal Democratic Party, Toshiro Nikai, to the Belt and Road Forum in Beijing. From then on, there has been increased cooperation between China and Japan.

Just three days ago, Japan and China signed an agreement to jointly invest in infrastructure projects in third countries. So, if two countries, which were not in a friendly mode, can agree on this higher level of reason of joint mutual interest for the benefit of third countries, I think this is a model for every country in the world. I hope that the Europeans will look at Japan. If Japan can change in this way, Europe should be able to do it as well.

Schlanger: Speaking of unfriendly nations getting together, look at the potential now between South Korea and North Korea.

I want to come back to Europe and the refugee crisis, because it's so central to the June 28-29 EU summit coming up. The refugee crisis seems to have hastened the confrontation taking place inside Germany, and I would like you to talk about that. But also, no one should lose sight of the fact that this isn't just a refugee crisis. The economic crisis continues; there are stupid and dangerous proposals being put forward by French President Macron and German Chancellor Merkel to increase the power of the Brussels banking bureaucracy.

The EU summit is coming up, Helga. What do you think will happen at the summit? And also, what are the chances that Merkel will survive?

Europe Needs Self-Reflection

Zepp-LaRouche: The mood in Germany—and we get this from all sides—is that Merkel should really go. It's time for her chancellorship to end; she has been there too long. The relationship between Horst Seehofer and Merkel has been poisoned for a very long time. The background is this: Seehofer, the chairman of the CSU (Christian Social Union) party and the Interior Minister, threatened to unilaterally impose controls at the German border which would mean that the Schengen Agreement [which abolished internal borders among France, Germany, Belgium, Luxemburg, and Netherlands] would be wastepaper, and with that, so would be the basis for the currency union, the euro.

Merkel met with Macron and insisted that she wants to have a European solution to the problem and not a German national solution. Even the mainstream media are mockingly saying that the chances that Merkel will get a European solution are slim. There are more than eight countries that refuse to accept refugees, and refuse to accept a quota for receiving refugees. *Die Zeit*, the Hamburg news weekly, wrote that the irony of the matter is that in this upcoming EU summit, Merkel will need the support of Greece and Italy for her European solution. These are the two countries that have been hit with the greatest amount of refugees. These two countries are where Merkel is the most unpopular—Merkel and Schäuble treated these countries absolutely brutally during the so-called euro crisis. The anti-Merkel sentiment in Greece and Italy is really quite large.

It's very difficult to say what will happen. It may be that Merkel will sell whatever result she gets as a Euro-

Bundesregierung/Bergmann

French President Emmanuel Macron (left) visits German Chancellor Angela Merkel in Berlin, May 15, 2017.

pean solution. In all likelihood, there will be some kind of bilateral deals that will include the horrible idea that I mentioned earlier—internment camps outside of the EU, which would be barbaric. If there is no agreement, it is still possible that by the end of the two-week ultimatum, Seehofer would unilaterally impose border controls in his capacity as Minister of the Interior, in which case, this would be insubordination against the Office of the Chancellor. If Merkel capitulates to that, her power is gone; but if she doesn't, her only option is to kick out Seehofer, who could then take the entire CSU out of the coalition with him. There are already polls indicating that the CSU would get 18% of the German vote, should they expand and become a national party.

This is all unworkable. No matter what combination you make—Merkel's CDU (Christian Democratic Union) party could take the Greens or the FDP (Free Democratic Party) into the government. But if they keep the policy, it will just be a prolongation of the crisis, and it will not solve anything.

There has to be deep reflection on the fact that the West is clearly crumbling. There are articles in all kinds of newspapers on this very subject. One article I found quite noteworthy was in the Austrian paper *Der Standard*, a liberal paper. The article says that the West completely missed its chance after the collapse of the Soviet Union. The United States was, then, the only superpower. The West gambled that moment away by plunging into abso-

lutely barbaric wars, in the Middle East, and other places, which wars caused the refugee crisis and many, many other problems, and, now, the West has lost.

There is a very interesting story this brings to mind: It's called "The man and the wife in the vinegar jug"— it's the *Essig-krug*, I don't know the word in English right now. It's about a man and a woman who live in an old, horrible house. A little bird comes and tells them to make a wish. The couple says, "We want a nice, big farmhouse, with many acres of land." Their wish is granted. However, they're not satisfied, and they ask for more, "We want a big villa in the city." They get that. Then their wishes follow quickly one after another: "Oh, that's not enough, we want to have a big castle, and we want to be King. That's not enough, we

CC/Mstyslav Chernov

Syrian refugees resting on the floor of the Keleti railway station in Budapest, Hungary, Sept. 5, 2015.

German Chancellor Angela Merkel, of the Christian Democratic Union, with Horst Seehofer of the allied Christian Social Union, during the 2017 election campaign.

want to be Emperor." They get all of this. Then, they say, "That's not enough: We want to be God." And then, everything vanishes. They are back in their old, horrible, little house.

The moral of the story goes to the chance missed by Western Europe and the United States: The West had the chance, with the crumbling of the Soviet Union, to change the world for the better. But, because of the limitless greed of that group of nations, and their limitless power-seeking activities, they messed it all up. So, I find this nice, little fable to the point.

More fundamentally, the West should really reflect on what has been going wrong with the neo-liberal, left-liberal, neo-con, geopolitical model. Why is the Asian model so much more attractive to many countries? Why is the Asian model so much more concerned with the common good of the people? China is rising because the Belt and Road Initiative is absolutely the biggest infrastructure project in history, with a clear focus on the common good. We must find some thoughtful people in the West, who are willing to enter into dialogue on what *is* necessary to correct the present policies. I think there has been much too little reflection and serious thinking about what *is* going on. If people just insist on keeping the status quo of the neo-liberal establishment, the West will crash against the wall.

Given the fact that the Singapore model exists, I encourage all of our listeners to engage with us, to become members of the Schiller Institute, to participate in our activities, and strengthen such an international dialogue. Such dialogue and debate is extremely necessary, it's urgent. The potentials in the world situation are also very hopeful, because changes are already happening in a positive direction.

More European Integration Unlikely

Schlanger: Speaking of changes, the fact that the Austrian national daily *Der Standard* did what it did, even though it's three decades behind you, Helga, it's good that it made that comment.

Also, coming up at the EU summit, there's the question of what will be brought in by the new Italian government and Austria. The leaders of those two countries have been talking about getting rid of the sanctions against Russia, and also favor openness toward China. Do you think they will have much of a voice at the EU summit?

Zepp-LaRouche: The Italians clearly have learned from what happened to Greece. When the Tsipras government was voted in, it went to Brussels and tried to revolutionize the whole process, and got smashed! It got smashed by a combination of the EU, the other European governments, and the European Central Bank. I think the Italians will probably play it more carefully. I do not think there will be a similar process as there was with Greece.

Remember, Italy is not Greece. Italy is the third largest economy in Europe. There are also all these other governments that want Europe to move in a different direction: Spain, Portugal, the Balkan countries, the East European and Central European countries, Austria, and Switzerland are all on a different trajectory. I don't think the policies of Macron and Merkel in favor of a Eurozone budget will find any majority. Söder, the new minister-president of the Bavarian state government, said that he absolutely rejects the idea of a Eurozone budget; it would just means paying more to have another budget, of which Germany would have to pay a large proportion.

I think this idea of imposing more European integration now, at a point when almost all the governments are questioning the merit of the Maastricht Treaty process—I think this will not happen. That's my modest prediction.

Now We Can Influence History!

Schlanger: Let's hope some of them will take up your proposal on the Singapore model.

I want to get back to something you brought up earlier: the idea that President Trump has been somewhat freed by the breakdown of the Mueller investigation.

Special Counsel Robert Mueller is moving desperately—jailing former Trump Campaign chairman Paul Manafort, revoking his bail, and moving against Roger Stone, claiming that he was the WikiLeaks Russia connection. But at the same time, there's the report of Inspector General Michael Horowitz; there's more coming out in the Congress. How much longer do you think this dual situation can continue, with the allegations of collusion and obstruction, when all of the allegations are falling apart?

Zepp-LaRouche: There are signs that some Congressmen are moving forward aggressively. Next week, Peter Strzok will be forced to testify in Congress. I think many of these people connected to the Mueller investigation could face criminal charges, fairly soon.

C-Span

U.S. Department of Justice Inspector General Michael Horowitz testifying on how the FBI and DOJ handled its investigation in 2016 of former Secretary of State Hillary Clinton's emails.

Unless this happens, and the whole situation gets straightened out, the danger remains very high. It's not yet time to relax in the certainty that things are going in the right direction. The same Democrats and the same mainstream media that were silent when Obama (and before him Bush), during his two terms as President, was conducing these so-called "humanitarian wars," in which the worst kinds of atrocities were condoned— these same Democrats and media are now yelling and screaming against Trump because of this border question and the plight of children and families. The hypocrisy of these screamers is enormous!

They had called for a national demonstration this coming Sunday. Trump has now issued an order mandating that these families should stay together, with their children. The border police had questioned if all these children really belonged to these adults, because this had been a longstanding problem which started about four years ago under Obama. The human traffickers had figured out that they could send lots of children, and they did. At that time Obama slammed down as well.

I think this whole situation really needs a grand design. When you have a messy situation—which you now have here—sometimes you have to go to a completely different level—that is exactly what Trump did in Singapore. Having done that, in his incredibly good level of approach reflected in his statement in Singapore—"The past does not have to define our future," making clear things can be changed—I think he needs to take that kind of an approach toward this whole situation. The Muellergate affair should come to the point where the responsible people are brought to justice for their illegal acts.

The even bigger picture is the need for a grand design. Trump really has to move away from this building trade war, and move toward cooperation with Latin America, with China, and with Russia, and bring the United States in, as an integral part of development projects in Africa, Asia, and the Americas. Were he do that, I think the world would find itself in safe waters in a very short period of time. Since it is within reach, I can only repeat my appeal: Help us, and move with us, because this is the time we can all influence history, which cannot be done when everything is going along quietly along quiet roads. But in such times of turmoil, the whole world is changing; at such moments in history, interventions can be made if you have the courage, if you have love for civilization, and if you have a vision of what to do. Join with us, and help us turn this situation around.

Schlanger: I encourage all our viewers to go to the Schiller Institute New Paradigm website and get Helga's statement, "History is Now Being Written in Asia! The EU Summit Must Follow the Example of Singapore!" Circulate this statement, create a ruckus around it. Let's get that debate going!

Helga, thank you very much for joining us this week, and we'll be back next week.

Zepp-LaRouche: Yes, till next week.

The Empire Plans to Knock South Africa Out of BRICS with a Bloodbath

by Ramasimong Phillip Tsokolibane

June 24—The British Empire is exploiting an ominous and worsening crisis in South Africa (a crisis caused by the failing London and Wall Street financial system itself) to induce a bloodbath here, to effectively knock South Africa out of the BRICS and tighten the Empire's hold on our country.

The Empire hates the BRICS association of nations—which brings South Africa together with China, Russia, India and Brazil—and is desperate to destroy it. The BRICS is a major feature of the New Paradigm, in which nations are cooperating for the rapid industrialization of all, and the elimination of poverty. China's Belt and Road Initiative, which is catching on fast in Africa, is another major element of the New Paradigm.

In Africa, the two iconic projects of this New Paradigm are the new standard gauge railways from Addis Ababa to Djibouti, and from Mombasa to Nairobi. But these are just the beginning. For example, construction of the Grand Ethiopian Renaissance Dam—the largest hydro-electric project in Africa, which will produce 6,450 megawatts of power—is two-thirds complete, funded by bonds purchased by the Ethiopian diaspora. The associated high-voltage line, funded by China, is already complete.

Form a mental image of the Empire's hatred of African progress: The governments of Zimbabwe and Ethiopia are among those in Africa most attuned to the New Paradigm. On June 23, both Ethiopian Prime Minister Abiy Ahmed in Addis Ababa, and President Emmerson Mnangagwa of Zimbabwe, in Bulawayo, narrowly escaped assassination at public events. The chances that this timing was a coincidence are slim. Rather, it was probably intended that their deaths would serve as the kind of "shock and awe" that was administered to the United States in the sequence of assassinations in the 1960s—President Kennedy, Malcolm X, Martin Luther King, and Robert Kennedy. The events of June 23 provide the proper image of what the BRICS and South Africa are up against.

Now British agent Barack Obama, the man who annihilated Libya, assassinated its leader, and attempted to turn Syria over to the ISIS terrorists, has been invited to South Africa by the Nelson Mandela Foundation—to dishonor the memory of Mandela by giving the foundation's annual Nelson Mandela Lecture in Johannesburg on July 17. La-Rouche South Africa and two Muslim organizations based in South Africa—CAGE Africa and the Palestine Solidarity Alliance—have called for the invitation to Obama to be revoked.

Wikipedia

Barack Obama, presenting his Nobel lecture after receiving the Nobel Prize in 2009.

The Obama Foundation, headquartered in Chicago, is not coy about its mission. It has, for example, Bernadette Meehan as its executive director of international programs. She was formerly a vice president of private banking at J.P. Morgan, then special assistant to Secretary of State Hillary Clinton, and then served on killer Obama's National Security Council.

On the South African side, the Nelson Mandela Foundation is headed by novelist Njabulo Ndebele, who spent years with the Ford Foundation in New York,

Vineyard in South Africa.

a foundation associated with regime change projects.

But there is more on Obama's agenda in South Africa than a lecture and a meeting with President Cyril Ramaphosa. He is bringing with him his friend—his former ambassador to South Africa—Patrick Gaspard, who is now the president of George Soros' Open Society Foundations, notorious for their involvement in regime change around the world. At the time of this visit, the Obama Foundation will convene 200 of Obama's chosen acolytes of the Young African Leaders Initiative (YALI) from around the African continent for five days of training and workshops in Johannesburg. The *New York Times* of April 23, in referring to this, said that "Obama is inaugurating his most significant international project as an ex-president."

Before reaching South Africa, Obama will visit Kenya to meet Raila Odinga (and President Uhuru Kenyatta). Odinga is the presidential candidate who *attempted to inaugurate himself as president last January, after Kenyatta defeated him in the election*, making himself a kind of "poster child" for regime change.

When Obama reaches South Africa, he will be stepping into a country in which he and others have already been at work to engineer a bloody conflict from the prevailing, difficult circumstances.

The South African Picture

A large but unknown percentage of all South Africans—but well over ten percent—live in shacks put together from assorted materials, oc-cupying land illegally around the cities where many of them have jobs. There is often no electricity and no running water; there are no street lights, no paved roads, and often only pit toilets. They are regularly driven off by the police, who demolish their homes. The price of urban land is sky-high.

The frequency of these events—and other poor people's confrontations, protests, and destruction of public property—is rising, as poverty becomes worse in South Africa.

The leader of Black First Land First (BLF), Andile Mngxitama, promotes confrontation and urges the shack dwellers to seize more land. Mngxitama was formerly a Ford Foundation Fellow in the Sociology doctoral program at the University of the Witwatersrand, the center of the Eddie Webster network of regime change specialists.

Julius Malema—leader of the so-called Economic Freedom Fighters, with 25 seats in the National Assembly—harangues large crowds with a racial pitch, encouraging the seizure of land, including seizure of farms owned by white South Africans. At present, farmland is not being seized, but the murders of white farm-

Abahlali members meet at the Foreman Road Settlement, eThekwini.

Above, Julius Malema, leader of the Economic Freedom Fighters, speaking at the 2018 State of the Nation Address debate in the National Assembly, Cape Town, Feb. 19, 2018. Right, Malema with Lord Renwick.

ers continue. Sometimes the farm family is tortured before being killed. Malema, who calls the whites "cry babies," enjoys the patronage of Lord Robin Renwick and the Royal Institute of International Affairs.

A right-wing Afrikaner organization, Suidlanders (Southlanders), is preparing to fight in a racial "Armageddon" in South Africa. It has sent its spokesman, Simon Roche, on tour in the United States to raise money for his organization.

In contrast, the largest association of shack dwellers, Abahlali baseMjondolo (AbM), led by its president, S'bu Zikode, is committed to nonviolence, and has repeatedly urged the government to make land available. Many of AbM's leaders have been assassinated—killings that are often paid for by property developers. But the call for land is not the right demand. It is not enough, and by itself it will feed into British intentions. AbM's leaders understand that land is not simply a market commod-

creative commons

BRICS leaders at the 6th BRICS summit in Fortaleza, Brazil. Left to right: President of Russia, Vladimir Putin; Prime Minister of India, Narendra Modi; President of Brazil, Dilma Rousseff; President of China, Xi Jinping; President of South Africa, Jacob Zuma.

ity; they should be asking for a larger, more comprehensive change in the economy (see my statement, "Will South Africa Destroy Itself, While the Bitch Queen Laughs at Our Stupidity?" immediately following this article).

This is all grist in the British imperial mill. The British plan is to use tumultuous disorder and bloodletting as the pretext for a multi-party "government of national unity and peace" that they can control. While South African commentators are talking about a coming "Arab Spring," it would actually be a bloodbath.

South Africa is the chair of the BRICS this year by rotation, as it was five years ago in 2013. The BRICS annual summit of heads of state and government—and associated events—will be held in Johannesburg, July 25-27. Nine other African governments will participate, along with Argentina, Indonesia, Jamaica, and Turkey, under the "BRICS Plus" concept. The BRICS association must accelerate its work for the sake of Africa and the world. Obama, his foundation, and his partners in crime—the Soros Open Society Foundations—must be exposed and defeated.

Will South Africa Destroy Itself, While the Bitch Queen Laughs at Our Stupidity?

by Ramasimong Phillip Tsokolibane, leader of LaRouche South Africa

June 24—It is time that we have a discussion of some important truths that many of our fellow citizens stubbornly refuse to address.

Despite great strides made by the previous administration, South Africa is not yet a fully sovereign nation. Under the able direction of President Zuma, we correctly moved to align ourselves with the emerging New Paradigm, coming from the east, under the principal leadership of China's President Xi and Russia's President Putin, through our involvement in the BRICS alliance and China's Belt and Road Initiative.

However, thanks to the manipulations of British assets and agents in our political and financial elite, we still remain with one foot in the institutions of the collapsing Western monetarist system, and we have refused to break our ties with the evil British Empire. While the New Paradigm is based on respect for perfectly sovereign nations, working peacefully together for the common aims of all mankind, the old, decadent London-dominated paradigm continues to impose cruel limits on our sovereignty, especially on our ability to invest credit and labor for a better future.

The most important thing we can do to increase the prosperity and happiness of all of our citizens—black and white, man and woman, rich and poor, and of all religions—is to step fully into this New Paradigm by breaking free of the ideological shackles that bind us to the British Empire and its immoral outlook, which divides us into false categories or classes, such as white and black.

The racist policies under which our nation has suffered, and from which in many ways we still suffer, are

CHOGM

Queen Elizabeth II (with handbag) at the Commonwealth Heads of Government Meeting in Trinidad and Tobago, Nov. 27-29, 2009.

a deliberate product of British manipulations. If we trace their origins, we see this in the policies of the British East India Company, and in its Dutch predecessor in South Africa, the Dutch East India Company. These are not "white" policies, but policies to subvert and control *both* black and white populations, for the benefit of the British (Anglo-Dutch) imperial elite, that are laundered as "white supremacist," and which engender a "black power" response. In that way, whites keep blacks down, and then blacks fight whites, resulting in a so-called "race war." I urge everyone who is falling into this trap, which is retailed by a British-dominated global media, to stop and think: Who benefits from all of this?

It is the truly disgusting, racist British imperial elite, who have used this method to divide people from their true self-interest and to keep people and nations under control. It is they who benefit.

At one point, the British and Dutch, and other imperial powers, openly used the whip, the bayonet, and the cannon. But always, lurking in the background just behind the uniformed soldier and colonial police, is the racist financial establishment, which issues the orders to the murderous and anti-human colonial administrators, and thus oversees the looting of the Empire's colonies.

The Second World War, and the leadership of the great American President, Franklin D. Roosevelt, forced a weakened Great Britain and the other European imperial powers to agree to set their colonies "free." But FDR, a true emancipator in the tradition of Abraham Lincoln, did not live to see the fully sovereign and prosperous nations emerge from colonial Africa that he intended. After his death, the British were able to subvert his intent through their "Winds of Change" policy of "enlightened" colonialism, under which nations were granted a nominal political "freedom," but were kept financially and economically tethered to the City of London and its Wall Street satrapy, thereby aborting their cultural and physical development.

Under colonialism, the British and the other imperial powers instigated wars with—and between—African monarchs and chiefs to destroy their ability to rule. They stole the Africans' lands by conquest, backed up by colonial law, to force Africans into virtual slavery on the farms, and in the enterprises and homes, of the colonizers. Then, following World War II, the theft of land continued by "legal" means, while yet more of the African patrimony was stolen using NGOs—especially the World Wildlife Fund of the super-racist Prince Philip and his Dutch accomplice Prince Bernhard—to set up so-called "game preserves" for hunting and other enjoyments for the rich, while denying the land to everyone else. Africa has thus been kept in a condition of perpetual, enforced backwardness and underdevelopment, as desired by London and Wall Street.

The British Hate Africa's Economic Potential

Enter China and Russia, and the BRICS alliance, which openly seek to unlock the vast economic potential of Africa, through credit for large-scale and other infrastructure and development projects. South Africa, with the only full-set economy on the continent—capable of making the machine tools needed for this new and great agro-industrial development—must serve as the engine for these projects, if they are to succeed.

President Xi Jinping of China and South African President Jacob Zuma shake hands at BRICS summit in Brazil, 2014.

Hatred of this wonderful potential lies behind a new British-inspired effort for "race war" in South Africa today, in response to South Africa's efforts to address the domination of its economy by what is misnamed White Monopoly Capital and the existence of large "white" land holdings.

The issue to be addressed is, how can South Africa rid itself of British imperial control of its economy? That is not a white vs. black issue, no matter how many people scream otherwise. By turning it into a white vs. black issue, various British operatives misdirect our population, and protect the continued control of our nation by London and Wall Street dominated interests and their allies inside our nation. If the right buttons are pushed, we will get a "race war," egged on by the fake news media sewers of the right and the left.

The way to fight the imperialists is by working through the BRICS alliance to accelerate the progress already underway under President Zuma's leadership towards our full incorporation into the New Paradigm. Our problem is that the new Presidency, under London and Wall Street asset Cyril Ramaphosa, has held back—even as South Africa prepares to host the BRICS summit next month. If the British, their flunkies, and their dupes have their way, we could find ourselves in the beginning a staged "race war" by that time.

As a patriot, I urge calm discussion of some basic truths:

The Radical Economic Transformation policy is flawed, because it does not consider what it proposes in the context of an overall agro-industrial policy for the nation.

If we do not have a defined agro-industrial policy actually in place, one that provides long-term, low-interest credit—that is, one unconstrained by London and Wall Street and their institutions of control, such as the IMF—ownership of land will not deliver the dreamed-of benefits, and, what's worse, the expropriation of land would play into the British "race war" trap. The question of land ownership can only be discussed in this context.

It's the Empire, Stupid!

There is no approach to the challenge of creating greater prosperity and opportunity for all South Africans, black and white, that does not begin by addressing the reality of British imperial control of what should be a sovereign economy. That control works through agents and assets in South Africa, but their power does not even derive from their domestic wealth or assets, but via their service to the London-centered imperial elite.

These agents' power does not solely derive from property titles, and it is simplistic to believe that merely taking away their property will solve the problem of endowing our people with national sovereignty. That said, our government, in the name of sovereignty, does have both the right and obligation to confiscate and re-assign property titles whose ownership obstructs and subverts the national interest, and to determine fair compensation, if any.

A property title, as properly understood, is a *contingent* right granted by a national economy that does not establish an unlimited right to do whatever the holder wants, but requires that it serve a positive national purpose. When that title is abused, or used against the national interest—when land or other property is held back from development and misused against the interest of the people, which sovereign government is constitutionally bound to protect—the title holder can lose his or her title rights and the title can be transferred to someone else, under lawful due process.

For example, large amounts of land owned by the mining companies could most definitely be expropriated without compensation—or rather, without further compensation—through an orderly procedure. The companies have had plenty of compensation already.

Alongside the question of property titles, there is much to be done to make land serve a function. Urban and peri-urban land must have infrastructure—water, sewerage, roads, electric power. Owning farmland does not mean much if there is no infrastructure and you can't get a bank loan to buy farm equipment, seed and fertilizer. Land transfers must not be to the detriment of productivity. Land expropriation will only work if long-term, low interest credit is available.

Placing the emphasis solely on expropriation and redistribution of property titles, puts the cart before the horse and opens the door to Brutish inspired "class warfare" and racial conflict. By placing the issue of redistribution in the proper context of a national agro-industrial development policy, and debating that policy, we will expose the racist British Empire and its assets as the enemy of our nation's progress.

What we propose is to give blacks—and whites—the opportunity for productive, meaningful lives. Blacks must have ownership of their own destiny; the shackles of their economic oppression must be removed. That oppression is a relic of the continued presence of the British Empire. Let us forget about the false term "White Monopoly Capital" and call it by its proper name—the British Empire and its dying financial system. That the representatives of this imperial elite are white, and have names such as Rupert, Gray, and Oppenheimer, is not as important as that they collectively serve British imperial interests.

It really does not matter whether you are white, black, or purple—if you serve the British Empire, you are enemy of the future of our nation. The British are fond of pointing to all the blacks they have trained to run commerce and political life. All they have done is create a caste of Royal-rump-kissing traitors, whose ideas have infected our leadership, and through the media, our people.

Such people have committed and are continuing to commit serious economic and other crimes against our nation and our people, black and white. They should be exposed and prosecuted, and if convicted, enjoy years behind bars. This is what a nation must do to obtain its sovereignty.

These are the issues that we must address. This is what I and the LaRouche movement intend to make sure happens. In the end, you are either a patriot, or an asset of the British Empire. Many of you call yourselves patriots, but you wave the banners and repeat the slogans devised by the British Empire to foment "race war." The time has come to wise up to their game of divide and control, and choose which side you are on. The future of our nation and of all Africa, depends on your choice.

ramasimongt@hotmail.com

Trump 'Unbound': Door Opens for U.S. To Join the New Paradigm

by Harley Schlanger

June 22—The worst nightmare of those British and U.S. intelligence operatives responsible for the fraud known as "Russiagate" appears to be on the verge of coming true. Reports coming from Trump administration sources confirm that planning for a Trump-Putin summit is well-advanced, possibly to take place as soon as the second week of July, either before or after the NATO summit in Brussels on July 11-12. National Security Council (NSC) spokesman Garrett Marquis tweeted on June 21 that at the end of June, National Security Advisor John Bolton will "travel to Moscow to discuss a potential meeting between Presidents Trump and Putin." The Russiagate scandal was launched precisely to prevent Trump from developing a collaborative relationship with Putin, which would break with the anti-Russian policy of his predecessors.

The *Times of London* immediately reacted with a nasty article citing numerous unnamed British officials as being upset by the news. A "senior western diplomatic source" said a Trump-Putin summit would cause "dismay and alarm," while a Whitehall source told *The Times*, "Everyone is perturbed by what is going on and is fearing for the future of the alliance," referring to NATO. The Times charges that Trump's call at the G-7 meeting for reinstating Russia had the effect of "wrecking Mrs. May's efforts to further isolate Mr. Putin after the Salisbury poisonings." Not surprisingly, *The Times* did not mention that

CC/G7

G-7 Heads of State Summit in Canada, June 8-9, 2018.

the British charge against Russia in the Skripal affair remains unproven, and was one of a series of provocations by London against Russia and Putin, to deter a Trump-Putin get-together.

Similar anti-Trump, anti-Putin comments have been heard in the U.S. Ned Price, a former spokesman for the NSC under Obama, tweeted on June 21 that for Trump to meet with Putin "before or after the NATO summit is a slap in the face to the alliance.... And that's probably just as Trump intended." Members of both parties in the Congress have criticized Trump for moving to fulfill his campaign pledge to achieve a good, positive collaborative relationship with Putin. Senator Charles Schumer, the Senate Minority leader, attacked Trump for his call at the G-7 summit in Quebec to bring Russia back into

Left to right: French President Emmanuel Macron, United Kingdom Prime Minister Theresa May, and President of the European Commission Jean-Claude Juncker.

the G-7, saying he is "turning our foreign policy into an international joke." Republicans have been less outspoken than Schumer in attacking the decision to work with Putin, but many warn that Putin cannot be trusted—which is the same line many elected officials have—including Schumer and Republican Senators such as Marco Rubio, Bob Corker and John McCain—in criticizing Trump for meeting with North Korea's Kim Jong-un, and for pursuing a collaborative friendship with China's President Xi Jinping.

Congressional anti-Russian hysteria was behind the August 2017 vote in the U.S. House and Senate for sanctions against Russia over unproven allegations of election meddling. The votes of 419-3 in the House and 98-2 in the Senate were condemned by Trump, but he signed them anyway, as a veto would have been easily overturned. Despite positive meetings with Putin on the sidelines of summits in Hamburg and Vietnam, the President has been constrained, until now, by the Russiagate investigation which has targeted him, his family and his campaign, to prevent him from building on those encounters.

Trump 'Freed'

The constraints now seem to have been broken by Trump, who is acting as "a sovereign U.S. President," in the words of Helga Zepp-LaRouche. In a statement released on June 17, "History Is Now Being Written in Asia—The EU Summit Must Follow the Example of Singapore," she hailed the breakthrough of the Trump-Kim meeting, pointing to it as proof that formerly "unfriendly" nations can make historic agreements, in the new optimistic strategic environment shaped by the "New Silk Road Spirit." This model could be employed, she wrote, to change the direction of Europe, away from the failed policies of the European Union, based on the axioms of the old paradigm, which have been in place for the last three decades, with U.S. presidents playing a leading role in their enforcement.

It was Trump's engagement with China, Russia, South Korea and Japan, which opened the door for the process which led to the success of the Singapore summit. The first major step in this direction was Trump's decision to take the U.S. out of the Trans-Pacific Partnership (TPP) free trade agreement, a central part of President Obama's "Asia Pivot," which was designed to undermine the emerging role of China, and to counter its Belt and Road Initiative (BRI). The adoption by many world leaders of the Chinese "win-win" approach of pursuing policies of mutual

President Donald Trump (right) speaking with North Korean leader Kim Jong-un, at their June 12, 2018 meeting in Singapore.

benefit, is demonstrating that peace and prosperity can result from this kind of engagement.

At the same time, the visible unraveling of the fraudulent narrative of Russiagate, has given Trump room to follow through on his own diplomatic initiatives, in spite of at-times strident opposition, even within his administration. This is the theme of a June 15 article by Susan Glasser in the *New Yorker* magazine, on Trump's decision to proceed with the summit with Putin. "There's no stopping him," a senior administration official told her. "He's going to do it. He wants to have a meeting with Putin, so he's going to have a meeting with Putin."

Michael Horowitz (right), Inspector General of the Department of Justice, being questioned by Rep. Mark Meadows, North Carolina, at a House hearing on the IG report on the Hillary Clinton email probe.

Glasser compares Trump's resolve to meet with Putin with his decision to meet with North Korea's Kim. It was "a major policy move carried out in spite of his advisers, not because of them, and with little genuine support from either Republicans or Democrats." He "has increasingly acted like a President unbound," she concludes, "undeterred by the troublesome politics that would make a Putin summit unimaginable at this point in any other Presidency."

Russiagate Hoaxsters Now on the Defensive

The release last week of the report by Department of Justice's (DOJ) Inspector General (IG) Michael Horowitz on corrupt practices by officials of the DOJ/FBI in their handling of Hillary Clinton's use of a private email server is further enabling Trump to break out of containment. The charges that Russia "meddled" in the 2016 U.S. presidential election, and that Trump and his campaign "colluded" with the Russians, were hatched with collaboration between the highest levels of British intelligence and U.S. intelligence community officials under President Obama. The narrative was prepared, as admitted by the FBI's number-two counterintelligence official, Peter Strzok, to "stop" Trump's election, or to provide an "insurance policy" were he to win.

Strzok's comments were made in a text message to his mistress, former FBI attorney Lisa Page, and are part of the evidence of DOJ/FBI bias against Trump contained in the IG's report. Referring to the text saying "we'll stop" Trump, the IG wrote it is "not only indicative of a biased state of mind but, even more seriously,

implies a willingness to take official action to impact the presidential candidate's [Trump's] electoral prospects." The texts "demonstrated extremely poor judgment and a gross lack of professionalism." He concluded that the communications are "deeply troubling" and "cast a cloud" over the Clinton investigations. The IG's report did not include an investigation of DOJ/FBI improprieties in Russiagate, though it should be noted that many of those involved in the Clinton case, including Strzok and Page, were also assigned to Russiagate, and the two were initially part of special counsel Mueller's team. Further, Strzok was the FBI liaison to CIA Director John Brennan, who has been identified as the leading U.S. player in initiating the Russia/Trump investigation. Strzok and Page were removed from Mueller's team when the existence of their texts was first revealed by Horowitz.

In addition to Strzok and Page, a deputy to disgraced former FBI Deputy Director Andrew McCabe—who is awaiting possible criminal charges for his role in leaking classified intelligence on Russiagate to the media — three other FBI officials were identified as exhibiting extreme hostility to Trump.

As to the actions of former Director of the FBI James Comey, who was fired by Trump, the IG found Comey to be "insubordinate" in his handling of the Clinton email case, and in violation of protocol, as he "usurped" the authority of the Attorney General. The report says "we find it extraordinary that ... Comey engaged in his own subjective ad hoc decision-making," and his actions have "negatively impacted the perception of the FBI and the Department [DOJ] as fair administrators of justice."

The exposure of Comey's corruption has severely damaged Mueller's case against Trump for "obstruction of justice." Trump's firing of Comey is justified by his abuse of his office, and not as an effort by Trump to shut down the investigation. However, despite the evidence produced, the IG's report shockingly concludes that Comey was not "politically biased in his actions."

This conclusion was lambasted in Congressional hearings on June 19-20, as numerous Republicans pointed to the absurdity of any claim that personal bias did not impact decisions made in pursuing the phony charges against Trump. For example, Horowitz was challenged by Rep. Mark Meadows (R) to look into charges that FBI agents altered documents related to the Clinton email and Russia probes. Horowitz told the Committee he had received information on this, and would follow it up. If confirmed, it could wreak havoc on Mueller's investigation, as there is already evidence that some FBI agents involved in the questioning of Trump's first National Security Advisor Michael Flynn, who pleaded guilty to "lying to the FBI," were not convinced that Flynn had lied. Peter Strzok, who was involved in the interrogation of Flynn, has agreed to appear before the House Judiciary Committee to answer questions.

Trump has repeatedly referred to this investigation as a "witch hunt," leading his opponents in both parties, as well as the mainstream media in the U.S., the U.K. and Europe, to attack him as "paranoid" and "delusional." His repeated calls for a summit with Putin, to shift away from a post-Cold War provocative containment of Russia to a new era of cooperation, have been cited by the anti-Trumpers as evidence of his debt to Putin. They demand instead that he inflict further punishment on Russia, in the form of crushing sanctions and NATO deployments on its borders. According to these opponents, any concession to Putin, or even a meeting with him, proves the charges that Trump owes his election to the misdeeds of the Russian President, or that he is subject to blackmail by him—all based on the deceitful and salacious memos drafted by former MI6 operative Christopher Steele.

The initiating role of British intelligence in the scandal is now in the spotlight. LaRouche PAC issued a petition and memo calling for an end to the "Special Relationship" between the U.S. and the U.K., and a

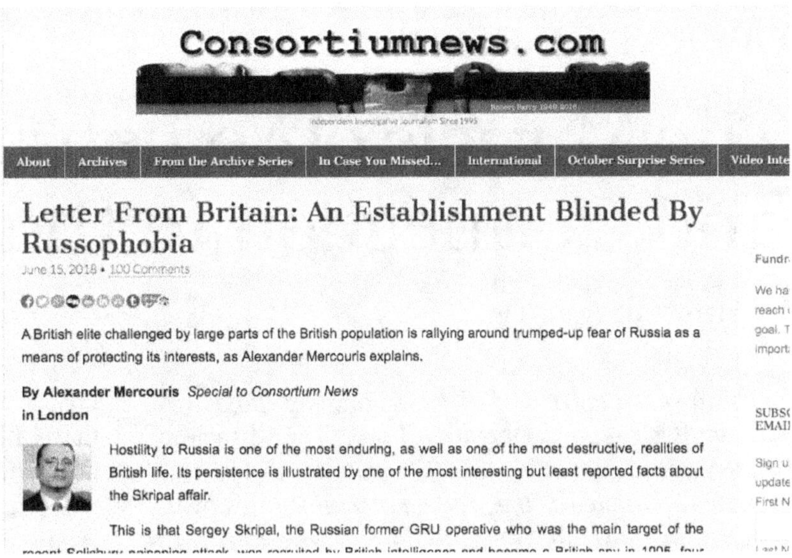

declassification of all documents relating to contacts between the intelligence agencies of the two nations. This in particular aims at the role of anti-Russian officials John Brennan, the former CIA director, and James Clapper, Obama's Director of National Intelligence, who both played leading roles in launching Russiagate, and continue to attack Trump and Putin, now as "commentators" on mainstream news outlets and on op-ed pages.

LaRouche PAC's demand that the British role be investigated is being taken up increasingly in non-mainstream publications. Indicative is an article by Alexander Mercouris on June 15 under the headline "Letter from Britain: An Establishment Blinded by Russophobia," published by *Consortium News*. He opens by writing, "Hostility to Russia is one of the most enduring, as well as one of the most destructive realities of British life." After detailing the collusion between MI6, GCHQ, and other British institutions with the CIA and FBI, he concludes that this hostility is not only a "constant and enduring fact of British political and cultural life," but it "appears to be a predominantly elite phenomenon."

The strategic direction chosen by President Trump, of collaboration with the emerging economic powerhouse associated with the BRI, offers the prospect of consolidation of a New Paradigm, and the defeat of the dangerous war and financial speculation paradigm of the City of London and their American neocon, neoliberal followers. Trump's initiatives have opened the door for the New Paradigm. As Mrs. Zepp-LaRouche concluded in her memo, "Needed now, are the people to make it happen."

The Miracle of Yemen's Reconstruction and Connection to the New Silk Road

by Hussein Askary

This is a summary review of the original, 86-page Arabic-language report, Operation Felix: The Miracle of Yemen's Reconstruction and Connection to the New Silk Road, *which was the product of a joint effort by the Schiller Institute, the Yemeni General Investment Authority (YGIA), and Swedhydro Consulting (Sweden). The project was coordinated by the Yemeni New Silk Road Party and its founder, Fouad Al-Ghaffari. The report's author is Hussein Askary, Southwest Asia Coordinator for the Schiller Institute and a writer for* Executive Intelligence Review. *The report was released at a seminar in Sana'a on June 6, 2018. The original Arabic version is available to download free of charge at the website of the New Silk Road Party of Yemen.*

The reconstruction of Yemen, after the currently ongoing, destructive Anglo-Saudi war of aggression is concluded, will require a miracle. But that is exactly what this report proposes. The time of miracles is upon us. Many miracles have been achieved and many others are underway. A new era in the history of mankind has dawned under the leadership of the BRICS nations (Brazil, Russia, India, China and South Africa), and the launching in 2013 of the Belt and Road Initiative (BRI) by China's President Xi Jinping. These two developments have opened the gates of history to a new and just world order.

China's miraculous industrialization process over the past two decades, lifting 700 million of its people out of poverty, is a strong indicator of this new process. The fact that China has offered its technological capabilities, know-how, and financial resources to partners in the developing world to replicate this miracle, is a strong motivation for the Yemeni people and leadership to opt for the highest levels of ambition.

This is the context within which Yemen could rise and achieve its own miracle. As the Yemenis managed to achieve the miracle of resisting the most vicious and powerful military forces, they can—with the same measure of success—achieve the miracle of reconstruction. The reconstruction miracle will naturally be more difficult than the military one, but it will be more joyful, and will bring together all the citizens of Yemen—men and women from all possible parts the country and from all different backgrounds as a unified force for the good of the entire nation.

The reconstruction process will unify the people of Yemen in the exact opposite way as the war of aggression—and those behind it—sought to divide them. It will preserve the dignity and grace of the Yemeni individual and his and her cultural identity with the same force that their enemies used in attempting to destroy that identity through efforts to eliminate its people and destroy their beautiful cultural and architectural heritage.

The Republic of Yemen enjoys a unique geographical position at the intersection of the land-based Economic Belt of the New Silk Road and the

Maritime Silk Road—that is, the Belt and Road. Yemen can become the bridge between Asia and Africa, and between the Indian Ocean and the Mediterranean, and thus a key component of this giant development project, while benefitting from it at the same time; in the words of Helga Zepp-La-Rouche, "making Yemen a pearl in the necklace of the New Silk Road."

Yemen played a similar role in ancient history when it mastered the trade routes, called "the incense and gum routes," and many powerful nations from east and west set sail and drove their camel caravans in its direction, seeking trade and exchange of knowledge. The ancient Greeks and Romans called Yemen "Arabia Felix," because it was perceived as a prosperous and happy nation. Today, Yemen enjoys great human resources, as most of its population are children and youth under 30 years of age, making it a young society capable of progress and continuity into the future through comprehensive and long-term visions and economic plans.

Yemen also has abundant natural resources and a diverse climate and topography, making it suitable for integrated agro-industrial development. Lacking in Yemen is what American economist Lyndon LaRouche calls "the economic platform" of basic infrastructure, to lift all these resources to higher levels of productivity and bring into being their latent great potential. Such a raised economic platform will allow Yemen and its people to take control of their economy, their resources, and their future.

Operation Felix

"Operation Felix" proposes a project for the reconstruction of Yemen on the basis of accumulated knowledge and lessons drawn from successful reconstruction models achieved by other nations in recent history, such as Germany after World War II, or after major economic disasters such as the Great Depression in the United States in the early 1930s, or nations that managed to evolve from poverty into powerful and prosperous industrial ones, like South Korea and most recently China.

From the scientific-economic aspect, the full report

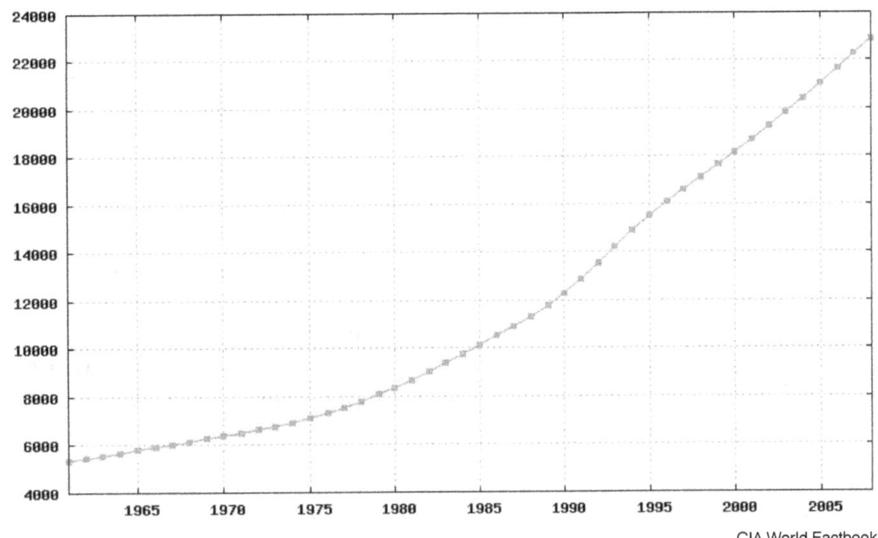

Population growth in Yemen beteen 1960 and 2010 in thousands of individuals. Today the population stands at 27 million.

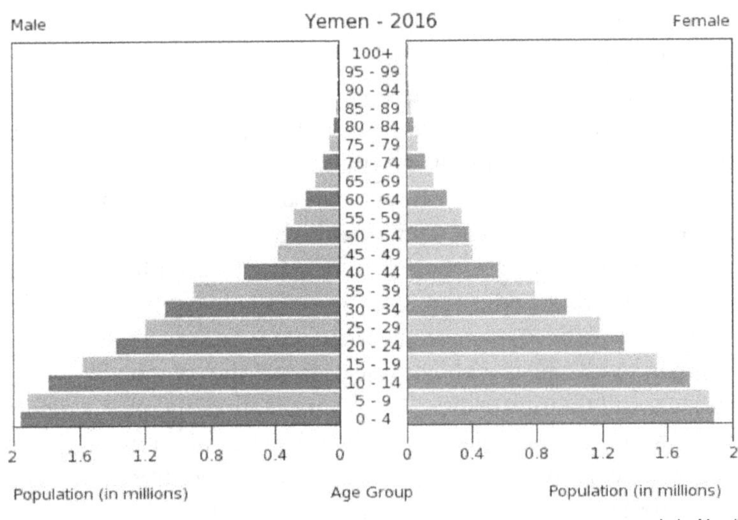

The population pyramid of Yemen shows a very young nation with an amazing median age of 19.2 in 2015, which is projected to be 29 years in 2050.

relies on the Science of Physical Economics, as defined by LaRouche, and not on the monetary or rentier/physiocratic theories and methods that were imposed between the early 1980s and 2014 and earned Yemen the nickname, "the poorest country in the region." LaRouche's "Metrics of Progress" have become a subject of study among certain groups of Yemenis in the past three years.

Our report makes it clear from the outset that the Operation Felix plan is not based on the idea of reconstructing Yemen's economy to restore it to its previous conditions before the war of aggression was launched in March 2015, nor to its state before the 2011 popular revolt, because that state of economic affairs was a disaster, as explained in detail in Chapter 2. The intention is to provide the "economic platform" for a prosperous and progressing nation, and connect it to the BRI. It also deals with Yemen as a single, unified country, with a centralized government and a unified and integrated plan for the reconstruction of the country as a whole.

When projects everywhere in the country have the same standards and metrics, such as in the transport, power, and communication sectors, from the remotest point in the north to the far south, they will be achieved much faster and at lower cost, in comparison with small projects each carried out locally with different standards. Integration of the reconstruction and development process requires the establishment of a central "reconstruction authority," functioning under the Ministry of Planning, with branches or offices in every governorate in order to coordinate with the local administrations the planned projects and their priorities. The centralization and unification process is very important in light of attempts, both before the war, and now by the Saudi-led coalition, to divide Yemen into a confederation of six regions, encouraging separatism and tribalism.

Destruction of Economy Before the 2015 War

One important feature of this report is the description of the disastrous policies of the past 30 years, prior to the war, that made Yemen the poorest country in the region. Our reason for reviewing these policies and the conditions they created is to warn policy makers against the pitfalls of the economic and financial methods that have been dominant in the trans-Atlantic power structure and its clients/victims, and the prospect that when peace is achieved, there is a risk that the same economic methods will come back, disguised this time as "reconstruction aid."

A relevant phenomenon defined here is the "rentier state," defined by Hossein Mahdavy[1] as a state that relies almost solely on the export of its abundant raw materials in order to import its needs, with little attention paid to investments in improving domestic productive capacities. While Saudi Arabia, the Gulf states, and other OPEC nations are good examples of this, Yemen is an extreme example. In the decades that followed the the Republican revolution of September 1961, but especially under President Ibrahim Al-Hamdi, who launched a major local development process and the five-year plans of development in 1974, until his assassination in 1978 (by Saudi-backed elements), Yemen was on its way to achieving a promising level of modernization and development.

However, these plans slowed down after Al-Hamdi, and when Yemen discovered its crude oil reserves and launched its oil production and export in 1986, the state was suddenly awash with easily earned foreign currency. In 1987, the global crude oil price was in the U.S. $40/barrel range, lower than the very high levels of the early 1980s when the Iran-Iraq war had begun, but that was still a major income volume for a poor country. But when the Asian Crisis of 1997 hit the

Collapse of Health and Social Services			
	1990	2000	2014
Prevalence of undernourishment (%)	28.9	29.6	26.1
GDP per capita (U.S. dollars, purchasing power parity)	3,441	4,018	3,832
Underweight children under age 5 (%)	29.6	43.1	35.5
Cereals import dependency ratio (%)	69.9	78.6	81.2
Improved water source (% of population)	66.3	59.9	54.9
Food exports (U.S. dollars, millions)	30	32	180
Food imports (U.S. dollars, millions)	613	719	3,682
Below poverty line (%)	n.a.	33	54

Trade Deficit in Food Items			
Net trade (U.S. dollars, millions)	1990	2000	2014
Cereals	−251	−302	−1,917
Fruits and vegetables	−16	−13	−146
Meat	−27	−62	−217
Dairy products	−62	−78	−285
Fish	14	16	193

Some basic economic indicators for Yemen show the extent of the disastrous economic and social conditions in the country even prior to the start of the Saudi coalition's war on the country in 2015. Source: FAO

---

1. Hossein Mahdavy, "The Pattern and Problems of Economic Development in Rentier States: The Case of Iran," in *Studies in the Economic History of the Middle East*, ed. M.A. Cook (Oxford: Oxford University Press, 1970).

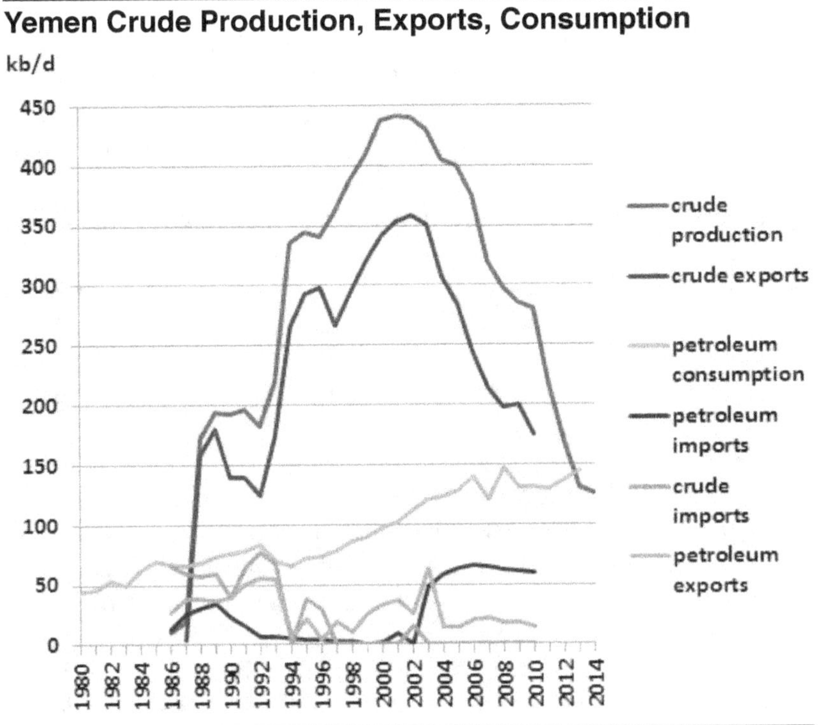

Yemen Crude Production, Exports, Consumption

Here, "petroleum" refers to refined products, such as diesel and other fuels, in addition to petrochemical products.

global economy, the oil price dipped to the range of U.S. $20/barrel. It did not recover until after September 11, 2001 and the invasion of Iraq that followed in 2003, reaching the range of U.S. $100-120/barrel. However, following 2007-2008 financial crisis, the price collapsed again.

This factor made Yemen a hostage to the volatility of global prices and its almost total reliance on exports of oil to finance its needed imports of food and almost every other commodity. Another disaster hit the economy when the production capacity of crude oil from Yemeni wells started to shrink in 2002, as new exploration and production projects were not considered profitable by international oil companies in a stagnant world market. Foreign debt was on the rise and more loans were required to cover the trade and state deficit. In the early 1990s, Yemen had lost its main financial partners: Iraq, now under a criminally harsh UN economic sanctions regime following the 1991 Kuwait war, and the Soviet Union, which disintegrated later that year—a factor which left Yemen on its own to face the combination of aggressive neighbors and the twin vultures of the IMF and World Bank.

The Yemeni government, under President Ali Abdullah Saleh, was already in the clutches of the IMF in 1995, after the destructive civil war of 1994. The Yemeni government started receiving conditional loans from the IMF and World Bank from 1995 on, through the usual "structural adjustment programs,"[2] forcing the state to privatize its corporations, lift all state subsidies for food and basic commodities, fire tens of thousands of state employees, and open its domestic market to competing foreign goods through radical free market policies that killed whatever existed of domestic production. Needless to say, Yemen was no longer allowed to build infrastructure or industries, nor to support agricultural projects, and practically lost its sovereignty over the economy.

The "private sector" was supposed to carry the burden abandoned by the state, but that was impossible in such a poor country. A massive privatization campaign of state-owned enterprises ensued, allowing the corrupt leadership of the country to enrich itself by transfer of ownership of these assets. Despite the dire food situation in the country, especially after the global food price crisis in 2008, Yemen was encouraged to increase exports of cash-generating crops, such as fruits and vegetables, with Saudi Arabia and the Gulf countries being the main market. With no support for, or protection of, domestic cereals production, farmers switched to growing more cash-generating crops, such as fruits and vegetables, but more seriously to the Khat drug, consumption of which exploded in that period and increased even further later, creating additional economic, social and health problems for the society, especially for those in lower-income brackets. The fisheries sector was the only sector that received any significant investments, but that sector was dedicated not to providing food for the Yemeni people but for export markets.

All these factors made Yemen a net importer not only of food (80% of its cereals needs by 2014) and other consumer goods, but also of petroleum products, such as diesel and motor oil, as the state was discouraged from investing in building new refineries and petrochemical industries. Almost no major infrastructure

---

2. IMF, Enhanced Structural Adjustment Facility Medium-Term Economic and Financial Policy Framework Paper 1999-2001: http://www.imf.org/external/np/pfp/1999/yemen/

projects were launched, and all the advice and financial support the Yemeni government was given by the IMF, World Bank, and the UN was to concentrate on small projects here and there. Later, the Yemeni government was even forced to hand over control of its newly discovered gas fields in 2007 to foreign developers, among them the French company Total and the United States' Hunt Oil Company.

The Saudi War: the Planet's Worst Humanitarian Disaster

Chapter 2:2 details the consequences of the Saudi-coalition's bombardment campaign since March 2015, which specifically targeted infrastructure, industries, power and water utilities, and even agricultural production. By all legal standards, this bombing campaign qualifies as a war crime. The coalition has also imposed a total land-air-sea blockade on Yemen, preventing food and medicine from flowing into the country, and preventing people in need of emergency medical aid abroad from traveling, through the targeting of airports.

The statistics compiled by the Yemeni Ministry of Human Rights, corroborated by international humanitarian agencies, reveal a horrendous level of destruction and suffering.

By January 2018, there were 22 million Yemenis (70% of the population) who were in need of food, medical aid or shelter. Seven million were in acute need of food aid. 2.9 million children and women were acutely malnourished. Sixteen million lacked clean water and sewerage, leading to the explosion of a cholera epidemic. Seventeen thousand people died out of the 120,000 sick people who needed to travel abroad for emergency medical treatment, but were stranded by the closing of Sana'a's airport. Civilian victims, as a direct result of military operations, were 17,000 dead, mostly women and children, with an additional 24,513 injured. As for the indirect casualties, it is estimated that 300 civilians have died since March 2015.

Of the infrastructure, almost all power generation utilities have been destroyed. Most oil and gas production is stopped, except for a few fields controlled by the Saudi coalition. Airports, ports, bridges, and roads are being systematically targeted. Even fishermen and their boats have become targets. Many industrial facilities—mining, metal production, food processing, logistics centers, and dairy product plants—have been systematically targeted and destroyed. Even schools, technical education institutions, and universities have been tar-geted. Hospitals were not spared either.

Financially, the Saudi-controlled government of exiled President Abed-Rabbo Mansour Hadi, decided in September 2016 to move the Central Bank operations from Sana'a to Aden, which is under the coalition's control. This meant that the bank was no longer able to pay the salaries of millions of state employees in areas not controlled by the coalition, increasing the suffering of millions of families. Furthermore, the Central Bank was not able to facilitate trade transactions with foreign exporters of food, medicines, and other necessary commodities.

Reversing the Policy

1. Financing Reconstruction. As proposed in the full report, the reconstruction and development plan will start with the Acting President in Sana'a making a public statement, even before a ceasefire is reached, that the government of the Republic of Yemen is intending to launch a reconstruction process and a development plan for the nation. He will define the key priority projects and objectives of the plan, starting from the emergency action plan to rebuild the destroyed infrastructure; provide immediately needed food and medical aid; and invite friendly powers to participate in new infrastructure projects, defining the future connection to the BRI. However, he will immediately follow that by announcing, in the same statement, the establishment of a national reconstruction and development bank to finance the process.

For Yemen to be a truly independent and sovereign nation after this war, it will have to have its own credit-generating mechanism. The reconstruction and development process will require the establishment of a national development bank (tentatively called in our report "The Yemeni National Bank for Reconstruction and Development," or YNBRD) to finance the national projects in infrastructure, agriculture and industry. The YNBRD is to be owned jointly by the state (51% stake) and the citizens and private and financial institutions of Yemen (49% stake). Foreign governments and financial institutions may also subscribe to a limited share of the stocks or bonds of the bank. All grants and financial aid by friendly nations should be converted into deposits in the bank.

The YNBRD will be under the supervision and direction of the Finance Ministry and separate from the Central Bank of Yemen. The details of how credits are generated nationally by the YNBRD are treated thoroughly in Chapter 3:1, which makes reference to similar historical examples and the origin of this "national credit" system, as originating from the ideas of the first U.S. Treasury Secretary Alexander Hamilton in the young Republic of the United States of America.

The other, additional source of financing for reconstruction and development projects, especially ones requiring foreign technologies, machinery and involvement of foreign companies, is through export credit agreements with the nations whose corporations participate in, or export the necessary material for, the development projects.

One very good example from Yemen itself, is the 2013 China-Yemen agreement to finance the Aden Container Terminal Expansion project. That project was planned to be carried out by a Chinese company, being financed through a loan extended by the Chinese Ex-Im Bank to the Yemeni government. However, the project was not carried out because of the ensuing dangerous security situation. The intention was to make the Aden Container Terminal one of the largest ports in the region for transshipment, allowing Triple E-class Maersk super-large container ships to dock at the port. The agreement was signed November 2013, one month after President Xi Jinping announced the concept of the Maritime Silk Road of the 21st Century, which would make Aden and the other Yemeni ports key components of global trade and economic exchange.

The Yemeni General Investment Authority pre-sented to this author a list of projects (included as an appendix to the full report) in infrastructure, industry, agriculture, and fisheries, for which the Yemeni government is willing to cooperate with foreign investors on the basis of Build, Operate, and Transfer (BOT).

2. The Yemeni Development Corridors. The key

Graphic Representation of a 'Development Corridor'

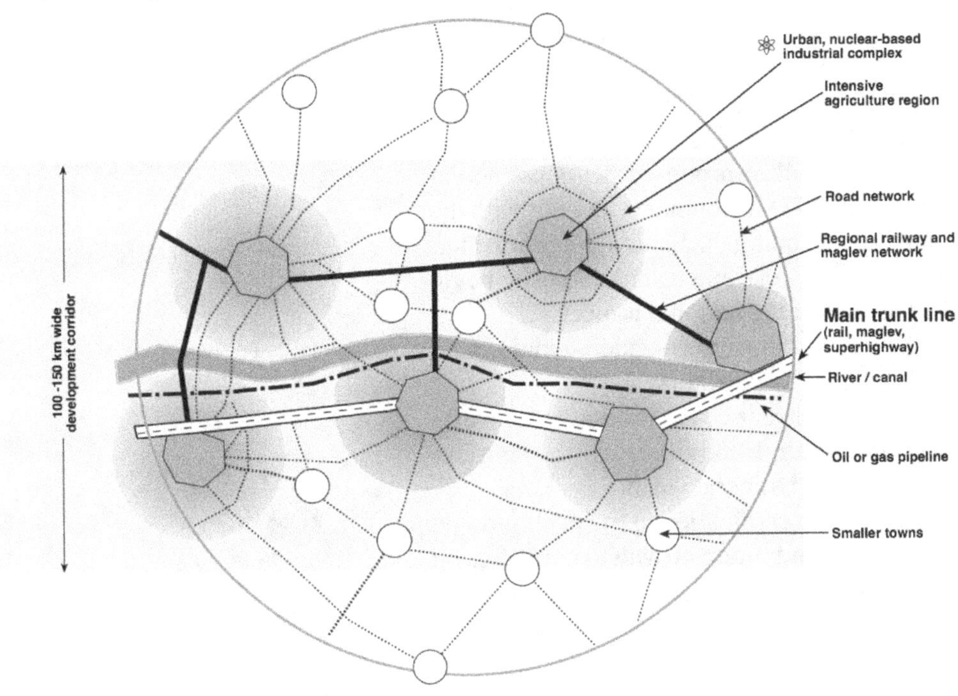

The Yemeni Development Corridors

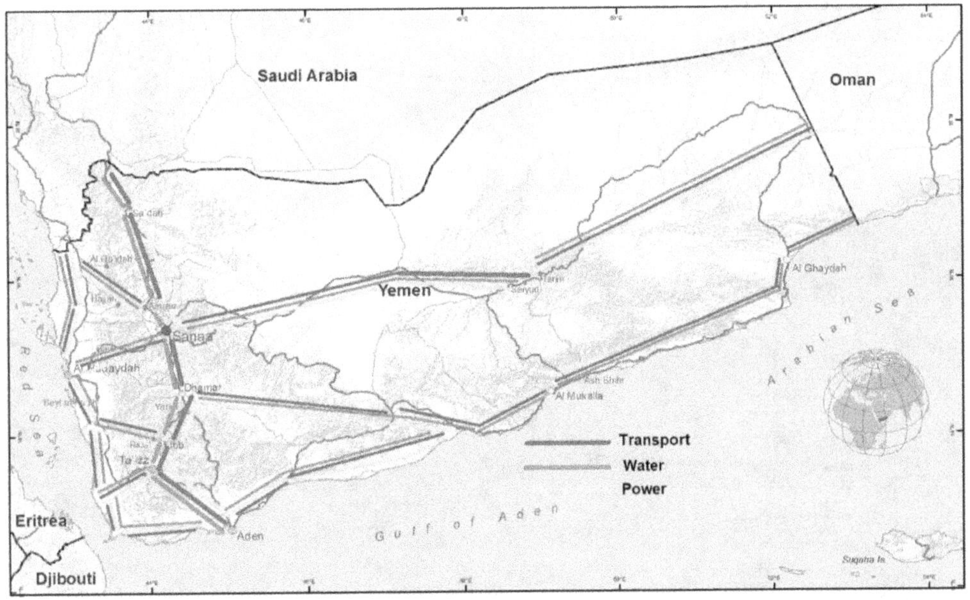

Hussein Askary

component in the report's reconstruction and development plan is the construction of the "Yemeni Development Corridor." After explaining LaRouche's concepts of the "Development Corridor" and the "Economic Platform," this author proposed the construction of the Yemeni Development Corridor with the main "spine" being the Sa'ada-Aden corridor, and the east-west extensions along it being the "limbs" of the national project.

Three factors were considered in defining the routes of the corridors:

(1) The current concentrations of population, agricultural activities, available water resources, and mineral wealth.

(2) The diversification of the demographic distribution and future growth to new areas on the western coast and eastern plateau, with both regions representing an untapped agro-industrial potential, in the mining sector, but most importantly in commercial agricultural activities, especially in the production of ce-

Population Density of Yemen (2005)

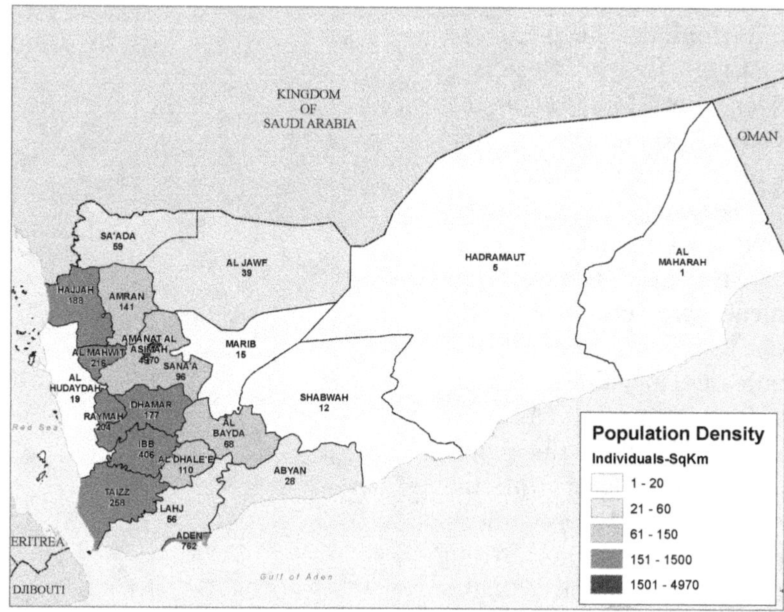

UN Office for the Coordination of Humanitarian Affairs

Eighty percent of Yemen's population live in the areas located along the proposed development corridors.

Yemen and the New Silk Road

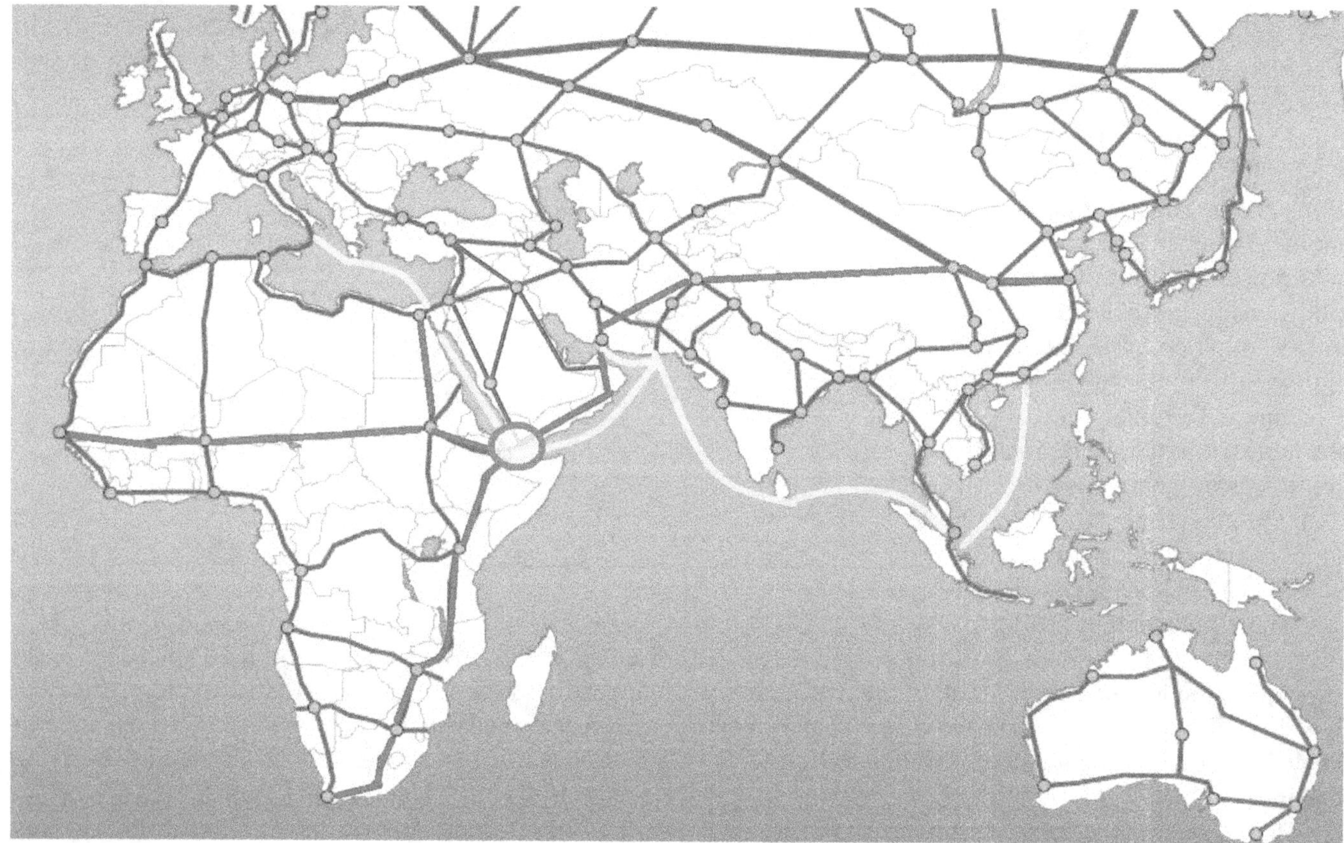

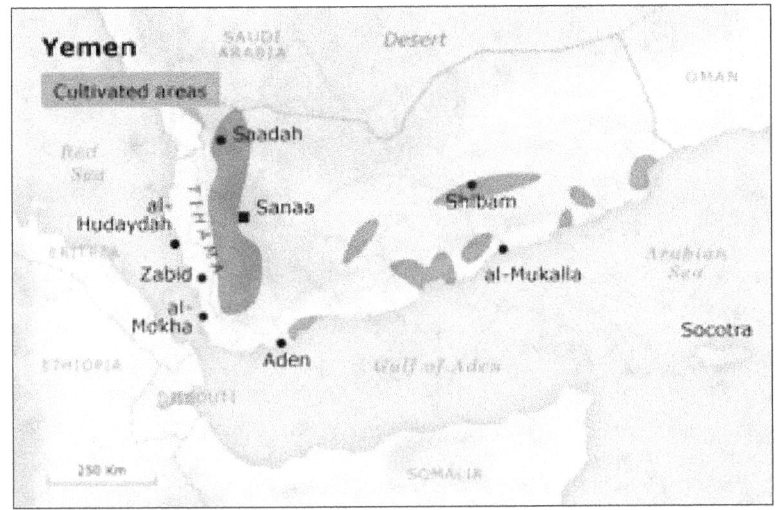

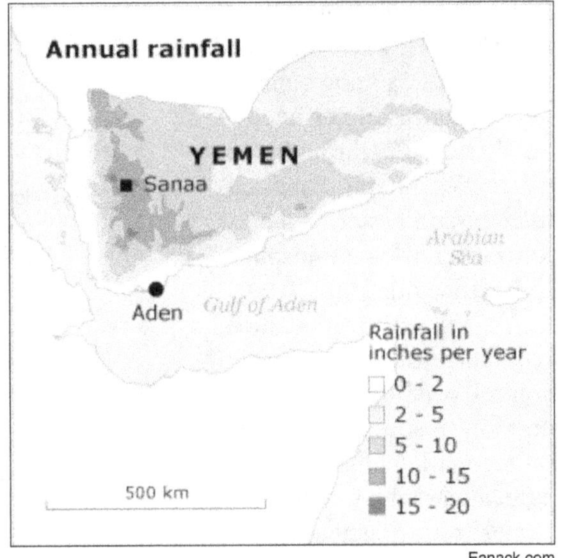

Fanack.com

The report proposes expanding agriculture to the eastern plateau and the coastal areas.

Fanack.com

reals to reduce and later eliminate the dependency on imports.

(3) Connecting to the BRI, on the land route to Oman and across the Hormuz Strait to Iran and Asia, and westward through a tunnel/bridge to Djibouti and Africa. The other connection to the BRI is through the main ports of Aden, Al-Hudaidah, and Mokha, where in addition to transshipment and logistics operations, new industrial parks can be built, benefiting from the proximity to international trade routes and the locally abundant human and natural resources.

The report references the tremendous developments taking place around Yemen, due to the BRI and China's different initiatives, such as the Djibouti-Addis Ababa railway, the Mombasa-Nairobi railway, the Lamu Port-South Sudan-Ethiopia Transport Corridor (LAPSSET), and many more projects that will transform Eastern Africa into one of the fastest growing regions. This is a great advantage for Yemen, which should consider that region as a great market, and also consider itself as a major logistics hub. To the east of Yemen, in Oman, the China-initiated Asian Infrastructure Investment Bank (AIIB) has already financed feasibility studies and preliminary work on a pan-Omani railway network extending from the Hormuz Strait to the border with Yemen, and new ports and industrial parks on the long coast of the Arabian Sea.

One interesting aspect of the developments taking place in Yemen's neighboring countries, Ethiopia and Oman, is that due to similarities in topographic and demographic characteristics, Yemeni policy makers will have ready examples of similar infrastructure projects, and will be able to examine the advantages, difficulties, technical aspects, and financing.

This author takes one example, comparing the proposed Sa'ada-Aden railway project to the standard-gauge Ethiopian Mekele-Weldiya-Awash railway, which is now under construction. The length of railway (622 km, compared to the proposed Yemeni project of 607 km) and the physical characteristics of the route, are strikingly close. Both will traverse mountainous areas reaching from 800 to 2,300 meters or more above sea level. In the case of the Ethiopian railway, the project required the construction of 31 tunnels with a total length of 20 km, 140 bridges (total length 20 km), and 1300 culverts (total length 40 km). The total cost of the railway is U.S. $4 billion. The Ethiopian state internally financed the first section with U.S. $1.5 billion, and obtained U.S. $2.5 billion provided through export credits from the export-import banks of China and Turkey, and Austria's and Sweden's foreign credit facilities.

Other Projects

Operation Felix envisions development projects for power, water, agriculture, and manufactures. Concerning water, we propose a national water management program, to include construction of a large number of medium-size and micro dams for rain harvesting and flood prevention, in addition to power generation. The Yemeni General Investment Authority (YGIA) suggested that U.S. $10 billion is required between 2019 and 2030 for construction of such dams on ten rivers in Yemen. In addition, a national network of water distribution and the regulation of groundwater exploration and utilization must be established. Besides the management of existing sources, new water resources need to be "created" through sea water desalination and climate engineering, such as ionization of the atmosphere to enhance rainfall.

As for power generation, report urges the state to regain control over the natural gas and oil resources, through re-negotiating the previous agreements with foreign companies, allowing the state to prioritize the production of electricity for domestic consumption before exports. In the short and medium term, natural gas, and the large, unutilized coal reserves of the country could be an appropriate response to the lack of power generation necessary for the nation's growth, as their construction takes less time (18-24 months) and are cost-effective.

However, for increasing and more efficient energy demand in the future, the Yemeni nuclear power program, which was proposed in 2007 but never started, must be relaunched. Nuclear power will not only be a key factor in power generation and desalination of sea water, but also will free the petroleum resources to be used in higher-value-chain products such as fertilizers, chemicals, and plastics, creating many industries in the country and employing tens of thousands of youth.

The industrial sector needs to be protected by abolishing the previous free market policies imposed by the IMF and World Bank. Through tariffs and customs, the state can protect the nascent industries that will be started by young Yemeni entrepreneurs to produce the needs of the domestic markets and for the global market, especially for the growing African markets. The development of infrastructure in Yemen, in addition to providing abundant power and water, will attract foreign investments in the Yemeni industrial sector.

In the agricultural sector, a new strategy for food security must be shaped, reversing the previous practices advised by the IMF/World Bank, UN and FAO that focused on small-holder subsistence farming. The new strategy envisions a dramatic vertical as well as horizontal expansion. The vertical implies supporting the Yemeni farmers through introduction of new irriga-

Fouad Al-Ghaffari (standing left), speaking at the seminar dedicated to launching the "Operation Felix" report, held in the capital, Sana'a, June 6, 2018. Seated at the far right is Engineer Khaled Sharafeddin, Deputy Director of the Yemeni General Investments Authority, currently acting director.

tion methods, development of new varieties of seeds, and applying fertilizers and machinery to farming. The horizontal expansion implies opening new land areas for large-scale commercial farming, especially of cereals, to secure the food supply of the nation and stop the bleeding of resources through reliance on imports. The state must once again assume its responsibility as the guardian of the food security and independence of the people of Yemen.

The Basis for a Lasting Peace

This author proposes that the government in Sana'a adopt the plan presented in the report as a key component in any peace and reconciliation talks between the different Yemeni belligerent parties, and that it be agreed upon in advance of any such talks. It should also be presented to each of the member states of the United Nations General Assembly, as a way of encouraging them to pressure the regional and international powers to bring about an immediate cease fire and push the national reconciliation and peace talks forward.

This proposal has the power and spirit, as has been expressed by most Yemenis who have reviewed it, to mobilize the various groups in the nation around a single, unified concept oriented towards a common goal in the future: to secure for their posterity well-being and prosperity. At the same time, it is a means of motivating the international community to consider the absurdity of continuing this war, and to accept the truth that the people controlling the government in Sana'a are not mere militias with power ambitions, but are statesmen with vision and knowledge. The responsibility to stop this genocidal war is upon every individual and every government in the world today. The vision for launching

'Sana'a Declaration' Adopts Schiller Institute Plan

In a powerful demonstration of the resilience and steadfastness of the Yemeni people in the face of the current Anglo-Saudi war of aggression, and the eagerness of the people and officials in Yemen to join the New Paradigm of international relations, a meeting was held June 6—at the headquarters of the Yemeni General Investment Authority (YGIA) in the capital of Yemen, Sana'a—to issue the "Sana'a Declaration," which declaration endorsed the 86-page Schiller Institute report, *Operation Felix: Yemen's Reconstruction and Connection to the New Silk Road*, authored by Hussein Askary, Southwest Asia Coordinator for the Schiller Institute.

YGIA acting director and deputy director, Engineer Khaled Sharafeddin, opened the meeting by thanking Askary and Mrs. Helga Zepp-LaRouche, President of the Schiller Institute. He expressed his full support for the proposals made in the report, and estimated that building the new economic platform, as proposed in the report, will require about U.S. $210 billion. Engineer Sharafeddin stated that the YGIA will work on two tracks with the government in Sana'a, (1) to translate the report into an action plan for the government, and (2) to thoroughly study all the infrastructure and financial proposals made in the report, in order to launch the construction process as soon as the war of aggression is ended. This work will begin immediately after the end of the Ramadan period of fasting.

Askary, the report's author, recommended that the Sana'a government present the report, to the United Nations and other international powers, to be included in peace negotiations as a key item to be agreed upon by all parties, in advance of political discussions.

The report, in Arabic, has already been sent to the leading figures in the Sana'a government and to key institutions internationally, including the Chinese and Russian embassies in Yemen. It is available to download free of charge from the website of the New Silk Road Party of Yemen, chaired by Fouad Al-Ghaffari.

a genuine reconstruction and development plan in Yemen—one that is in harmony with the new paradigm of cooperation in the world—has been defined.

Operation Felix
Table of Contents

Introduction
Chapter 1: The International Context
    The rise of the BRICS system and the collapse of the trans-Atlantic system
    What is the BRICS?
    What is the Belt and Road Initiative?
Chapter 2: The National Economic Context
    Before the war of aggression: The problem of the rentier economy
    During the aggression: The destruction of the basic infrastructure and creation of the humanitarian crisis
Chapter 3: Reconstruction
    How reconstruction of a destroyed economy can be financed
        The Hamiltonian national credit system
        "The Yemeni Bank of Reconstruction and Development": A proposal
    Proposed projects for Yemen
        The concept of "the development corridor"
        The "Yemeni Development Corridors"
            Transportation: The Yemeni main railway (Sa'ada-Aden) and extensions
            Power
            Water management
            Agriculture and fisheries
            Manufactures with appendix (projects proposed by the Yemeni General Investment Authority)
Chapter 4: Levels of the Operation
    First level: Emergency plan for rehabilitation of destroyed infrastructure, emergency aid to the population and youth employment, using Franklin D. Roosevelt's Civilian Conservation Corps as a model
    Second level: Negotiations with friendly powers on building a new economic platform
    Third level: Connection to the New Silk Road: Yemen as the Belt and Road bridge between Asia and Africa
Conclusion
Recommendations

You're Human! Do You Know What That Means?

by Robert Ingraham

There is a great deal of confusion about what it means to be a human being. The human identity is one of magnificence, beauty and great creative power. At this historical juncture, it is necessary to reassert what mankind is capable of accomplishing.

* * *

June 25—Today, the human species, of which you and I and all of us are members, is presented with perhaps the greatest turning point in human history. A moment of great change—change which will affect the lives of each one of us—stands before us. Greater than you would dare imagine. This is not an exaggeration. It is right in front of us.

As this is being written, nations and peoples from every corner of the world are coming together around the vision of a New Paradigm for peace, cooperation and economic development. This already involves more than one-half of the human race. The conditions of life for hundreds of millions of people are being uplifted. Water projects, energy projects, transportation projects, schools, hospitals and other modern facilities are being built all over the world. Despair is being replaced by hope, and people's lives are being changed for the better.

The driving force behind this dynamic is the China-created Belt and Road Initiative. Please, don't be stupid enough to fall for the line that "China is trying to take over the world." China is doing precisely what America used to do; it is building great projects. The many, many sovereign nations that have joined with China in these efforts, have done so as partners, not underlings, and these construction projects have created millions of jobs and great opportunities. We, in the United States—

A Chinese engineer with his Kenyan colleagues at a construction site of the standard gauge railway in Mombasa, Kenya.

Xinhua/Pan Siwei

as well as the people of Europe—could join this effort. We could begin building too. The door is wide open.

Yet, most Americans take little or no notice of any of this. It is as if it didn't exist. Almost no one talks about it.

Some might blame this failure to recognize what is right in front of us on the lying news media, others on the dismal state of public education. Others, still, might once again resurrect the overused outrage about "corrupt politicians in Washington." None of this is particularly useful, or even true. The problem is not that "someone out there" is "keeping us in the dark" about these great developments. No one is forcing ignorance and apathy upon us. We are doing it to ourselves.

You see, we have a problem. We now have a world situation which is the most hopeful, and with the greatest potential for human advancement, than at any time since the assassination of John F. Kennedy, now 55 years ago. This is actually the greatest moment of your entire lifetime. What transpires in the weeks ahead will affect the future for all of us. It will affect your future, and the future of your children. Yet, the majority of our people do not recognize the existence of this stupendous opportunity.

The Invisible Enemy

The problem we are dealing with, the enemy we face, is not in Washington, or London, or Beijing, or Moscow, or in the news media. It is not "out there." It is, as Shakespeare insisted, in ourselves. We have a great enemy, but it is not one that most people recognize. The enemy is our culture. Not someone else's culture: our culture!— that which defines how we think, what we believe, and what we attach our emotions to. Culture is not something "external" to who we are. From the moment we are born, to our last day on earth, we breathe in the spores of this culture. It shapes everything about us; and even if you rebel, and begin to denounce the flagrant degeneracy of what flows from Hollywood or San Francisco, the cultural octopus defines what you think can be done about it. We are all part of the culture, and the axioms of the culture determine how we think about what is possible.

First successful flight of the Wright Flyer, by the Wright brothers, Dec. 18, 1903.

America was once a nation that "built things." Our heroes were people like the Wright Brothers and Thomas Edison. Europe, as well, can point to a heritage of great minds and leaders. Where is all of this today to be found? Where is the impulse to create that which is new, that which is revolutionary, that which will benefit mankind? In our current culture—and in the views of your friends, relatives and co-workers—how much value is placed on the development of creativity? How much time and effort is spent—in child-rearing or even just friendship—in creative investigation?

Thomas Edison with "Edison effects" lamps.

The culture of today's trans-Atlantic society is almost devoid of any comprehension of what it actually means to be a human being. The self-identity of people—their own sense of what their life could be or how their actions might affect the future—has shrunk. The creative spark which carried the human race forward for thousands of years, from Plato, through the Renaissance, and into the space age, is today almost non-existent in the trans-Atlantic world. This is not an exaggeration. It defines the crisis in Western society.

What has been destroyed is any notion of what it actually means to be a human being. This is particularly true for those born after the murders of Martin Luther King, and John and Robert Kennedy. The joy of discovery, optimism for a better future, the excitement which once pulsed through the minds and hearts of Americans as Neil Armstrong headed for moon—all of this has been largely lost, and human passion is now directed toward the most banal, the most cynical, and the most self-destructive.

Do you think what is being said here is an exaggeration, or irrelevant? Look at what people do today for "entertainment." Look at the TV shows; look at the movies, look at the video games. It is all the excrement of a society with a death wish. If you have stomach enough, consider that the top most-visited sites on the Internet are all pornography sites. Protest all you want, but this is now who we are as a people. The poison of pleasure-seeking existentialism in America and Europe is omnipresent, swirling about us, engulfing us, and asserting everywhere that individual human existence is meaningless. Pessimism reigns. Human beings who are enslaved by such self-imposed cultural and mental chains, can not act for the future, because they lack any truthful basis for hope.

Certainly, there is goodness in every human being, and thousands of acts of goodness take place every day. We are human, and despite what the culture demands, it is in the nature of all humans to be good. But as the culture decays, the goodness grows weaker and is dragged downward, as if by a quicksand which no one can see or explain.

Will You Be a Victim?

This total destruction of American and European culture didn't just "happen." It didn't just "evolve naturally." And it is no accident. Since no later than 1914, the magnificent cultural heritage of Europe and the United States has been under siege. The culture with which the people of America and Europe are now victimized, is the end-product of more than a century of deliberate moral and intellectual debasement.

People used to believe in human progress, in the beneficence of human civilization. In truth, this is the underlying intention of the Preamble to the Constitution of the United States. Two 20th century world wars, followed by more than 40 years of a "cold war" which threatened human extinction through thermo-nuclear annihilation, destroyed most of that optimism.

The British Empire—the empire which most people refuse to believe still exists—created and then took advantage of these catastrophes. For more than a century, through certain mouthpieces such as Bertrand Russell,—and many others—the British elites have hammered at the Platonic-Renaissance conception of the human identity, determined to obliterate it. Human progress is the enemy of empire, of rule by the few, and if you destroy hope for the future you can more easily keep people in chains, much as tens of millions of

European societies are now under the diktat of a cultural regime that demands a morally-indifferent hedonistic human identity, a bestial identity, one grounded in sensual appetites—one which has no commitment to a more productive future. This is now proclaimed by nearly everyone as axiomatic human nature. It is everywhere, battering people with the non-stop drum-beat that you are just an animal.

It is the cultural mass-lobotomy of our people, as if the higher notions of human purpose and destiny were cut out and left lying in a bloody tray in the operating room.

The damage that has been done is gruesome to behold. Take the case of young women in our present-day trans-Atlantic society. It would challenge William Shakespeare to compose such a tragedy. Today, young

Fanny Mendelssohn

Marie Curie

Rosa Luxemburg

Indira Gandhi

Americans today are kept in debt slavery—and other forms of slavery.

Unlike many well-intentioned but impotent American patriots, the British aristocracy has always understood that the greatest weapon in their arsenal is cultural warfare. They did it in India. They did it in Africa. This is what the universities of Oxford and Cambridge exist for—to devise cultural, philosophical and religious means to control people all over the world. This is why the birthplace for the non-science of "anthropology" was at these two universities: to develop ways of defining a false sense of the human identity and to spread these lies to universities in dozens of other nations.

The belief in science, in progress, in human creativity was to be eradicated. This has been going on for decades, as deliberate oligarchic policy.

The end product is what we see today. American and

women are victimized, almost from birth, with a pornographic self-image. Once we had women of great personal courage, such as a Fanny Mendelssohn, a Marie Curie, or a Rosa Luxemburg—individuals who fought tenaciously for a creative universal identity. Where is that commitment to the future today? Where is the courage to locate one's identity in the creative development of one's own mind? Today's culture is all about the body, all about the flesh. The effect this has had on high school and college age young women has been devastating.

Additionally, with the recent cult of polymorphous "gender identity," young women—as well as young men—are told that the primary choice confronting them is, "What sex do I want to be today?"—gay, straight, bi-sexual, trans-sexual, trans-gender, non-binary gender specific, trans-whatever. This is now how people self-define who they are—through sex. In earlier times, people could joke about this; but now it is the inescapable cultural paradigm in Europe and America.

Accompanying this downward plunge has been the staggering leap in the deliberate drugging of our people, to the point today that perhaps as much as a third of our population is under the influence of drugs. The picture presented by Sam Quinones in his *Dreamland: The True Tale of America's Opiate Epidemic,* is not only terrifying, it is all true. And it is only the tip of the iceberg for a population saturated in the regular use of heroin, Oxycontin, cocaine, methamphetamines, hallucinogens, marijuana, Adderall, Prozac, Xanax, Ecstasy, Ritalin, and other legal and illegal mind-altering substances.

The Future

This is all coming to an end. We are in the terminal phase of the system of oligarchic empire. The major financial institutions in London and on Wall Street are all *de facto* bankrupt, and the empire is now thrashing about and lashing out—an imperial system that can not possibly survive. The growing world-wide consensus in support of a New Paradigm for peace and development heralds an entirely new future for the family of Man, one in which individual human contributions—and life—will have a purpose.

As a people, we are now presented with a moment of great opportunity. A magnificent future beckons. Yet, the culture holds us in chains. What is required is a new spirit to animate our people—to animate ourselves. The necessary catalyst for such a transformation lies in the ability for growing numbers among us to begin to rediscover the joy, the power, and the potential of what it means to be a human being—to come to grips with a rigorous understanding of the magnificent nature of our species and the limitless potentials which lie within each of us.

Let's start at the beginning...

I. A Unique Species

Far more than 99 percent of all plant and animal species that have existed since life first appeared on Earth are now extinct. This includes not only microbial life from billions of years ago,[1] but mammals, birds, amphibians and marine life which appeared over the recent millions of years. Given the historical record of the evolution of our planet, it is accurate to say that all living species are foreordained to suffer extinction. All, except one. Only the human species has the potential to overcome the fate of other creatures—to continue as an ongoing living factor in the development of the universe.

It is worth thinking for a moment about the truthfulness—and the implications—of the above paragraph. Today, students are routinely taught that a human being is merely an animal, perhaps a "clever" animal, but one nevertheless bound by the restrictions which govern all biological life. Probably, most people believe some version of this, but it is utter bilge, and accepting such nonsense is the first step toward a denial of what your real potential is as a human being.

Humanity's brief, yet shocking, record speaks for itself. Since the first appearance of human culture two million years ago, all human beings have exhibited a quality of Mind that absolutely separates the nature of the human species from all other living creatures. Lies to the contrary, there can be no factual dispute to this reality. Humans are not animals.

The species-mortality which distinguishes all other creatures from mankind is to be found in their *subservience to nature*, i.e., they exist biologically and hereditarily *within nature*, entirely dependent on the conditions of life which exist at that moment in time. As the planet, solar system and galaxy change—sometimes in abrupt and cataclysmic fashion—these creatures possess no means to surmount those existential crises. Thus, "extinction events" have occurred again and again throughout the long history of our planet. The birth and passing of individual species are inseparable from changes wrought by galactic, solar, and terrestrial processes.

Whose Human is Human?

Extinction is not mankind's destiny! The human species need not suffer the fate of other living creatures. To arrive at the reasons why this is true, however, will require some concentration and mental work.

Unlike lower-ordered species, Man does not exist within nature. We are not controlled by nature or dependent upon nature. In fact, the long history of the human species is one which conclusively exhibits the human

---

1. There exists a growing body of evidence that life has been present on Earth from the beginning, over four billion years ago. This vindicates the view of Lyndon LaRouche that life has always existed, as an embedded principle, within our universe. More will be said as to the implications of this below.

ability to take mastery over nature, to develop and transform nature, or what Vladimir Vernadsky calls the *biosphere*.[2] Mankind possesses a power over nature which all other living creatures lack. At the same time, and with even more shocking implications, it is legitimate to say that *mankind does not exist even within the universe*, as if some heteronomic biological creature, buffeted about by "dead" inorganic galactic forces.

This may seem like a ludicrous statement to some, but consider that the relationship between the creative nature of the human mind and the processes which underlie the universe have been a subject that has been at the heart of human investigation for millennia. It was Plato who first explored this relationship in his discussions of the *One and the Many*. The same subject was attacked again by Nicholas of Cusa in his investigation of the *Minimum and the Maximum*. Later, Gottfried Leibniz took up the same challenge in his work on the *Monad*.

What Plato, Cusa and others investigated, and what they established, is that we do not live in a chaotic universe, but rather one governed by *principles*, and that these principles are lawful. Our universe is one that has progressed in a manner coherent with universal principles of harmonic, self-developing creation. It is not a dead Newtonian universe.

What is truly shocking is that the ongoing creation of such universal processes—the self-evolving nature of the universe itself—resembles nothing so much as a motivic thoroughly-composed, well-tempered polyphonic classical composition. The work of Johannes Kepler and Johann Sebastian Bach is absolutely definitive in this regard, and there can be no legitimate argument with what they discovered.

What is even more shocking—earth-shaking—is that the ability of the individual human mind to compose agapic well-tempered polyphony is the "proof of

Johann Sebastian Bach (1685-1750).

From a print in the British Museum.

principle," for it demonstrates conclusively that the creative discoveries of the human mind are in harmony with the nature of the universe itself!—and that in the case of the human species, this is both willful (full of will) and conscious. This is true physics, as defined by Lyndon LaRouche in his seminal essay, "Poetry Must Begin to Supersede Mathematics in Physics."

This is where the secret to the human personality is to be found. It is in investigating the harmonic and unfolding relationship between the individual human mind and self-organizing universal change that one must seek the truth about the actual human identity. The human mind is not *in* the universe; it is inseparable from a universal process of ongoing creating.

As Tony Papert wrote in a recent Preface published in *EIR*: "There is no abiotic universe of physics—there is only the one existing universe. In it, the principle of life and the principle of creative mentation are everywhere active, and Max Planck truly said that you cannot get behind or beyond consciousness, even in the smallest particle—if such particle were possible. This is the hylozoic monism of Plato and his successors."

Aeschylus put it this way, in words he assigned to Prometheus:

But of wretched mortals he [Zeus] took no notice, desiring to bring the whole race to an end and create a new one in its place.

Against this purpose none dared make stand except me—I only had the courage; I saved mortals so that they did not descend, blasted utterly, to the house of Hades.

As we move through this discussion, there will be much detail and many dates, names and physical examples given. The purpose of putting this section of the paper at the beginning is to situate everything that follows. Don't get lost in subsequent details; keep what is important foremost in your mind.

To be continued.

---

2. Vernadsky, Vladimir I., "Human Autotrophy," *21st Century Science & Technology* (Fall–Winter 2013).

JULY 18, 2000

On a Basket of Hard Commodities: Trade Without Currency

by Lyndon H. LaRouche, Jr.

Excepting the usual rogues and economics illiterates, influential circles around much of the world are reporting, with ever lessening hesitation, that the presently rotten-overripe, world monetary and financial system, is doomed to an early chain-reaction collapse. Increasingly, among relevant circles outside the U.S.A., world wide, the most notable questions include, how to replace the present global system, and with exactly what?

Consequently, increasingly bold steps in search for a replacement have been taken, in East and South Asia, trends in progress since Malaysia, under the leadership of Prime Minister Mahathir bin Mohamad, has persisted in the clearly successful use of capital and exchange controls. Recent weeks of persisting, desperate, and provocative actions, from U.S. Treasury Secretary Larry Summers and perennial Federal Reserve Chairman Alan Greenspan, have provoked similar discussions currently in progress outside of Asia. These steps point, increasingly, toward the emergence of regional systems of economic cooperation. Such regional efforts, if combined, could serve as building-blocks of the new world monetary and financial system, once the present International Monetary Fund (IMF) is either sent, mercifully, into bankruptcy-reorganization, or simply disintegrates, soon, of its own accord.

Among those studying the prospect of regional alternatives to the imminently bankrupt IMF, some leading economists have proposed that the precedent, of the former role of the 1945-1966 U.S. gold-reserve dollar in creating a system of fixed exchange rates, might be superseded now by revival of a new system of relatively fixed exchange-rates, which is based upon regional and other "baskets of currencies," instead of the former gold-reserve-based dollar. The presently most publicized proposals in that direction, are those which have come from among the "ASEAN Plus Three" group of nations in Asia, and, secondly, among important circles within continental western Europe. Similar discussions are in progress among the Organization of the Islamic Conference countries.

In some relevant, leading European circles, attention has been directed to both the IMF Special Drawing Rights (SDRs), and the European Monetary System (EMS) proposal launched jointly by France's President Giscard d'Estaing and Germany's Chancellor Helmut Schmidt, the latter during the late 1970s. It is useful to compare such, and kindred proposals with my own mid-1970s proposal for an International Development Bank (IDB), which attracted vigorously antagonistic attention from sometime U.S. Secretary of State Henry A. Kissinger, and related circles, at that time.

In today's relevant European circles, as elsewhere, it is generally agreed that what President Franklin Roosevelt's U.S.A. did, to organize a post-World War II monetary system, worked very well, most notably to the benefit of both the U.S. and western Europe. This system prospered until the aftermath of that fateful year, 1963, when Germany's Chancellor Konrad Adenauer was pushed into resigning, U.S.A. President Kennedy was assassinated, and France's President Charles de Gaulle continued to come under the corrosive pressure of assassination and other attacks, attacks which persisted through the tumultuous cultural

The "ASEAN Plus Three" group of nations is discussing a "basket of currencies" as a basis for protecting themselves from the bankrupt global monetary system. Writes LaRouche: "I disagree, although sympathetically, with the suggestion that a basket of currencies could be a successful feature of the urgently needed reform." He proposes a two-phased alternative approach. Shown here are (left to right) Japanese Finance Minister Kiichi Miyazawa (Japan is one of the "Plus Three"), Malaysian Prime Minister Dr. Mahathir bin Mohamad, and Indonesian President Abdurrahman Wahid (both from ASEAN member countries).

and economic paradigm-shift of 1967-1969.[1]

However, it is also emphasized among those who recognize the urgency of returning to the principles of the pre-1971 types of international monetary agree-ments of fixed exchange-rates, that the U.S. dollar of this year 2000, if compared to the prestigious U.S. dollar and economy which still existed while President Kennedy was alive, is a relatively shabby thing. In addition to that fact, the fear is, that under either a new U.S. Bush Administration, or a presently unlikely Gore alternative, the worth of the dollar would sink quickly to incalculable depths. In addition to those considerations, as relevant circles in Europe and Asia note, the most conspicuously stubborn current source of resistance to re-establishing a system of fixed exchange-rates, is coming from the U.S.A. itself. *For that latter and other reasons, it has been mooted that the needed, new monetary and trade system, should use a basket of currencies, as a replacement for the 1945-1965 role of the U.S. gold-reserve-denominated dollar.*

I agree that the model of SDRs could be a leading included feature of the required economic recovery measures; but, I disagree, although sympathetically, with the suggestion that a basket of currencies could be a successful feature of the urgently needed reform. Instead of the suggested basket of currencies, I propose the following two-phased approach to the establishment of the needed new, global, fixed exchange-rate monetary and trade system.

I propose, that we structure the discussion of these

---

1. For those who may have forgotten, the following highlights of the period from the August 22, 1962 assassination attack on President Charles de Gaulle, through the October 18, 1964 rise of the disastrous Harold Wilson as Prime Minister of the United Kingdom, are notable: • On October 22, 1962, President John F. Kennedy declared the U.S.-Soviet missiles crisis. • The October 28, 1962 establishment of France's Fifth Republic under de Gaulle, is notable. • There is the historic January 14, 1963 meeting between de Gaulle and Chancellor Konrad Adenauer. • Then follows the February 14, 1963 election of Harold Wilson as successor to British Labor Party chief Hugh Gaitskell. • A new assassination attack upon President de Gaulle follows on February 15, 1963. • The July 1963 unleashing of that Profumo scandal in Britain follows, which led to the October 18, 1963 retirement of Prime Minister Harold Macmillan. • On April 23, 1963, Chancellor Konrad Adenauer announces his intention to retire in the coming October. • On November 22, 1963 President Kennedy is assassinated.

This interval, from mid-1962 through the election of Harold Wilson, is the location of one of the great turning-points in the course of modern history. The 1968 assassinations of Rev. Martin Luther King and of Democratic Presidential pre-candidate Robert Kennedy, less than six years after the Wilson election, and during the approximately half-year following Wilson's Autumn 1967 unleashing of the first of the series of monetary crises leading into Nixon's destroying the old Bretton Woods system, in mid-August 1971, are not to be regarded as the inevitable aftermath of the 1962-1964 interval, but as developments greatly encouraged by what occurred during that earlier interval.

During the late 1970s, German Chancellor Helmut Schmidt (left) and French President Valery Giscard d'Estaing initiated the European Monetary System proposal, which is usefully compared with LaRouche's 1975 call for an International Development Bank.

Bundesbildstelle Bonn

EIRNS/Stuart Lewis

matters in the following terms. Let us agree, that, at the present moment, the agenda for proposed reforms, is organized implicitly around the notion, that the safe escape from the presently ongoing global financial and monetary disasters, is likely to occur only in two distinct, if overlapping, successive stages.

That is to emphasize the fact, that, since the tragic blunder adopted by the U.S. Government for the October 1998 Washington, D.C. monetary conference, that government has not only abandoned its earlier options for leading comprehensive monetary reform, but has entered into promoting, most stubbornly, a global financial hyperinflationary spiral, one which has become recently, analogous to that which led into the Weimar Germany commodity-price hyperinflation of March-November 1923.[2] The continued folly of the U.S. mon-

etary and related policies, since the October 1998 Washington conference sessions, aggravated by the conduct and catastrophic outcome of the recent NATO war against Yugoslavia, has ruined much of the U.S.'s former, pre-October 1998 diplomatic potential for playing a constructive leading role in global monetary reform.

Thus, in light of the monstrous degree of degeneration in both U.S. credibility and policy-shaping since October 1998, a feasible reform, if it is to occur at all, were almost certain to come in two successive, regional and global phases.

The first stage, as typified by the ongoing discussion among representatives of the *ASEAN Plus Three* association, is typified by the revival of the 1997 proposal, by Japan's E. Sakakibara, for an *Asian Monetary Fund*. Such a facility is intended, not only as a measure of defense against financial-warfare attacks by hedge funds and similar speculators. It is also aimed to promote urgently needed measures of hard-commodity forms of combined trade and long-term capital improvements among those Asian nations. In this first stage, we might foresee regional, somewhat overlapping, groupings of similar outlook appearing, and cooperating among one another, in various regions of the planet.

The second stage, would be the re-establishment of

---

2. As my associate Richard Freeman has documented the available, pertinent evidence, about the close of July 1923 the German authorities' use of monetary inflation to continue to meet reparations-related payments, produced a phase-shift in the ratio of rates of monetary emission to outstanding financial debt. This unleashed the wild spiral of commodity-price inflation which completed the destruction of the currency itself three months later. The launching of "wall of money" policies adopted jointly by U.S. Federal Reserve Chairman Alan Greenspan and present U.S. Treasury Secretary Larry Summers during the interval October 1998-February 1999, has recently produced a phase-shift between monetary and financial appreciations of the same principled form as the July-August 1923 German case. The recent escalation of inflation in primary commodities, such as petroleum, food, and in real estate, reflects the recent and continuing onset of movement in the direction of a

Weimar-style blow-out of both the U.S. dollar and the IMF system with it. [See **Figure 1**.]

The Collapse Reaches a Critical Point of Instability

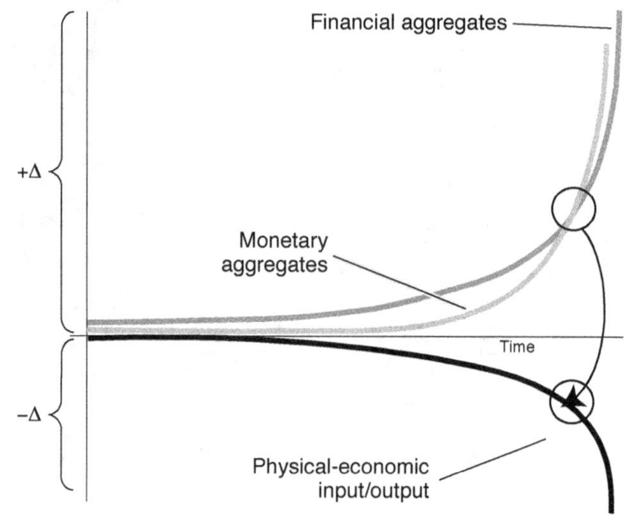

LaRouche's "Triple Curve" representation of an economy approaching collapse (a). With creation of money supply and of financial aggregates both growing at accelerating rates, the point at which the money-supply growth accelerates past even the growth of financial aggregates, is the boundary-point of entry into hyperinflation, as in 1923 Germany, or today's globalized economy. At that same point, the deterioration of the underlying physical economy (lower curve) also accelerates.

Weimar Hyperinflation in 1923: Wholesale Prices (1913 = 1)

(logarithmic scale)

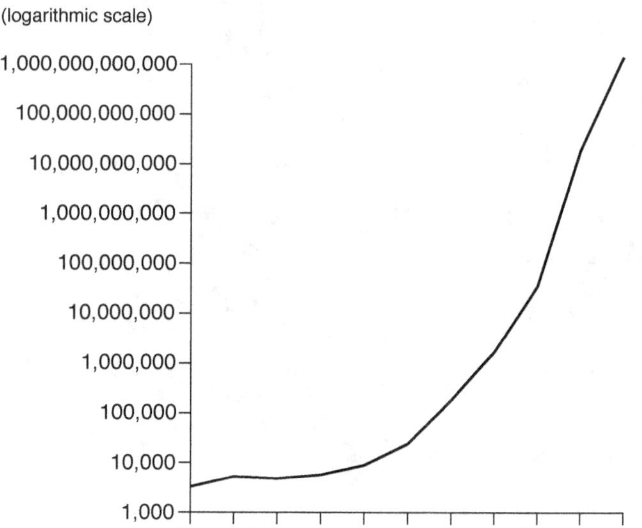

an effectively global monetary organization, featuring a return to fixed exchange-rates, to supersede the presently bankrupt IMF system. This second stage, would be a new monetary system, one assembled on the included initiative of participating regional groups of nations.

Therefore, examine the issue of "a basket of currencies" in light of the fact, that the two-phased approach to reform is, presently, the only visible prospect, if the world still has any favorable prospect of any kind, during the medium-term decades ahead.

The problem thus defined, is the following.

As long as the IMF system, and its related attributes exist in their present form, the attempt to use a "basket of currencies" as a substitute for the kind of role performed by the 1945-1963 U.S. dollar, is not a remedy, but a trap. Yet, the world can not wait until a general monetary reform occurs, to take certain urgent practical measures of defense against the worst effects of the presently onrushing global financial and monetary catastrophe. Therefore, at this stage, it has become essen-tial to institute *preliminary measures which operate entirely outside the supervision, or other control by the presently doomed, "globalized" monetary system.*

Hence, today, we need to see monetary reform presently as a two-step process. The first stage, is the emergence of regional blocs which operate either outside, or in parallel to the existing IMF system. The second stage, will be the crucial role of such regional blocs in constituting a replacement for the now already hopelessly bankrupt IMF system. In the interim, measures taken by regional blocs must scrupulously avoid the ruinous effects which must result, were such measures to become entangled systemically in the already doomed IMF system. A prudent man does not remain within a cabin of an already sinking *H.M.S. Titanic. The transition must be based upon economic values which exist independently of the present IMF system, and which can assuredly outlive that latter system.*

What Is in That Basket?

In assessing any selection of a basket of currencies, ask the question: "What are any among these currencies actually worth?" A scrupulously crafted answer would be: "Any combination of these currencies would be about as sound an investment as the German Reichsmark was at the beginning of July 1923." In short, the entirety of the present world monetary and financial system, is one gripped by an accelerating rate of financial and monetary hyperinflation in nominal financial assets; it is a system which is presently trapped in a critical boundary-state. We are presently at the verge of general disintegration of the present global system, including most leading currencies, excepting perhaps that of China and a few others, today.

All prudent policies must be designed to protect the credit of national governments from being dragged into the muck in which the present system will be surely buried. In short, the needed advice is: "Don't send good money down the sink-hole with the bad."

The crucial fact upon which all sound economic decisions are now premised, is the evidence which shows that the presently reigning financial and monetary institutions, are so hopelessly and profoundly bankrupt, that the world economy could not be saved without wiping several hundreds of trillions of current U.S.-dollar equivalent from the current, vastly hyperinflated, financial-asset-values account. In other words, outstanding financial claims must be brought implicitly into line with the world's present levels of an estimated hard-commodity valuation of the world's combined domestic product. Without such drastic reductions in nominal financial claims, no economic recovery from this on-rushing, biggest and deepest world depression, were possible. As much as the equivalent to $400 trillions in presently extant nominal financial assets of the world at large, will have to be either wiped from the world's accounts, or reduced, by reorganization in bankruptcy, to a mere fraction of their current nominal hard-commodity valuation.

Those claims denoted in such forms as financial derivatives, especially over-the-counter (OTC) derivatives, must simply be wiped from the books, categorically. Claims rooted in so-called "junk bonds" and kindred speculative fancies, must be treated similarly. Much of the international debt created, not by actual purchases, but by synthetic bookkeeping constructions, by administrative mechanisms of a floating-exchange-rate monetary system, must be simply cancelled. Large-scale write-downs in inflated financial value of real estate and other matters must occur. Even much honorable debt, including that actually incurred by sovereign governments, must be reorganized or rescheduled. In general, the total mass of financial claims must be pared down to those rates of aggregated debt-service payments which are consistent with a return to the economic-growth policies prevailing in western Europe and the Americas during the interval 1945-1965.

The principal concerns governing such financial and monetary reorganization, must be to resume and maintain levels of employment, consumption, and production, especially in hard-commodity categories of production and consumption, and to maintain rates of net growth, per capita, and per square kilometer, in hard commodity and related infrastructural qualities, which are consistent with what had been the converging policy-objectives of the governments of the U.S.A., France, and Germany, during the incumbencies of President John F. Kennedy, Charles de Gaulle, and Konrad Adenauer. In other words, the needed reorganization of the presently bankrupt international financial and monetary systems, must amount to a structural reform in composition of categories of employment, investment, and credit-flows, to return to goals and standards which are not inconsistent with the then-current operating objectives of those governments from that time.

Such seemingly drastic and sudden measures are not merely policy options. Such measures are now a precondition for the possibility for continuing anything deserving of the name "modern civilized life."

To those who have not yet thought through the relevant facts, it may seem extravagant to warn, that without such seemingly drastic measures of financial and monetary reorganization, without the kind of reversal of hard-commodity investment and production trends increasingly prevalent today, this planet will soon be plunged into a global dark age, into a downward spiral into sub-Saharan-Africa-like conditions, under which it were likely that world population levels would sink during coming decades, to well below a billion individuals. The alarming, but not exaggerated report of the new level of danger to all nations from global and regional infectious diseases, is to be read by all intelligent governments, and other relevant agencies, as a "marker" reflecting the presently diseased state of the world's economy at large.

This warning will not be considered an extravagant one, by any among those qualified specialists who have studied the physical and immediately related causes for the changes in the potential relative population-density (and life-expectancy levels) of Europe and the Americas since about A.D. 1500. If we consider the cumulative development of infrastructure and productive technology since the mid-Fourteenth-Century New Dark Age, we must recognize that the trends in policy-making under the IMF system since the mid-1960s, have

The 1963-68 Historical Turning Point

The postwar monetary system prospered, writes LaRouche, "until the aftermath of that fateful year, 1963, when Germany's Chancellor Konrad Adenauer was pushed into resigning, U.S. President Kennedy was assassinated, and France's President Charles de Gaulle continued to come under the corrosive pressure of assassination and other attacks, attacks which persisted through the tumultuous cultural and economic paradigm-shift of 1967-1969."

John F. Kennedy Library

Dr. Martin Luther King, Jr. (left) with Robert F. Kennedy.

Library of Congress Prints and Photographs Division

President John F. Kennedy (right) and his brother Robert, the Attorney General.

UN photo

British Prime Minister Harold Wilson.

reversed the long-term, net upward demographic trends in the direction of population-levels which had been reached, prior to 1966-1971, which had dominated long swings in European civilization during several preceding centuries. Without reversing sharply the accelerating down-shift in demographically relevant technology of investment and related practice, which has predominated under the IMF system since the mid-1960s, we have recently reached the brink of a global demographic catastrophe.

Such a catastrophe could be averted, even at this late stage, if leading nations of the world were to agree on measures which, in effect, bring the world's economic relations into forms of cooperation comparable to that shared between the U.S.A. and western Europe during the 1945-1965 post-war interval. It were sufficient to return to policies of practice comparable to what we in the U.S.A. and western continental Europe did rather well, if with some ups and downs, during those post-war years. Today, we must add the warning, that such cooperation be based upon a true, essentially global partnership with those nations which have been, until now, the continued victims of the legacy of colonialism, including the neo-colonial practices presently inhering in the common practice of the presently bankrupt IMF system.

The participation of a leading technology-exporting nation, Japan, in the ASEAN Plus Three process, if extended, in fact, into a more general cooperation throughout Eurasia, represents, at least approximately, a "full-set economy" base for high rates of gain in physically defined, per capita, productive powers of labor among all of the partners in such an arrangement. My hope is, that, despite the admittedly lamentable qualities of certain currently predominant preferences for U.S. Presidential pre-candidates, a sane government could emerge in 2001 out of the present, turbulent and mostly disgusting political process ongoing there at this moment, a government which will be a willing, cooperating partner in a global arrangement of the type which the aspirations of the ASEAN Plus Three group imply.

To reach that point in a timely fashion, certain preliminary steps are indispensable. To locate the required measures, we must take into account certain leading lessons from the period preceding the drift into the ruinous, presently bankrupt IMF "floating-exchange-rate" system. We must depart the disastrous changes in policy of the recent thirty-odd years, in preference for lessons to be learned from the successful experience of the 1945-1966 interval.

We are thus, in a condition, in which even many among the world's leading currencies will have to be either simply wiped from the accounts, or put through bankruptcy-reorganization under the authority of a new world system. In this transition, many presently leading currencies are to be, either, systemically reorganized, or, replaced by newly defined currencies and related credit-mechanisms. These currencies can be reorganized or created, so, only by reversing recent trends toward "globalization," by invoking the credit-creating authority of the perfectly sovereign nation-state.

It must be understood, that such reorganization is not the unthinkably radical proposal which some wild-eyed, pro-monetarist hysterics insist it is. As I have said: Either we do this rationally, by will, or the presently onrushing shock-fronts of global financial, economic, political, and social chaos will soon do it for us, whether we choose that outcome, or not.

We have been in similar conditions during the course of the just-concluded Twentieth Century; the present world financial and monetary crisis is deeper, wider, and bigger than anything seen during the Twentieth Century. Also, as in some relevant Twentieth-Century precedents, we shall be obliged to cancel bankrupt currencies from the accounts, replacing those by creating new currencies, new currencies to be established by the sovereign power of nation-state governments.

Admittedly, there is presently, hysterical resistance to any such reform. This is to be seen among politically powerful circles of financier-oligarchical interest, which represent today the same point of view on this matter as those Anglo-Americans, and others, who responded to the outbreak of the 1930s Great Depression, by joining forces to install and consolidate Adolf Hitler in power, during 1933-1934. The relevance of this point is made clear, by contrasting the proposed reform resolved upon by Germany's Friedrich List Gesellschaft in 1931, to the policies of the circles of such representatives of financier-oligarchical interest, as Britain's Montagu Norman, Norman's asset Hjalmar Schacht, New York's Brown Brothers, Harriman, and von Papen.

Today, the policies of the latter class of monetarist opponents of presently needed reforms, today's equivalents of the 1920s and 1930s Normans and Schachts, are represented chiefly, and exactly, by the circles of the Mont Pelerin Society, and such Mont Pelerin Society accomplices as Britain's former Prime Minister Margaret Thatcher, the U.S. Heritage Foundation, and the radical "free trade" fanatics in the U.S. Congress. If these latter, pro-financier-oligarchical forces prevail, as typified, in the U.S.A., by Larry Summers, Alan Greenspan, and the followers of pollster "Dick" Morris today, the world would soon see regimes and conditions worse than those which Europe experienced under Adolf Hitler's reign. *Here, on this point, lies, precisely, the immediate danger to all civilization, as typified by the U.S. Presidential pre-candidacies of Governor George W. Bush and Vice-President Al Gore.*

In this set of circumstances, policy-shapers should study more carefully the more deeply underlying principle behind the approximately twenty-year, 1945-1965, success of the post-World War II, Bretton Woods fixed-exchange-rate system, especially as that system operated in relations among the U.S.A., western Europe, and Japan. In this account, include attention to the fact that the way in which the system was implemented, after President Roosevelt's most untimely death, was vastly inferior to what the result would have been, both morally and economically, had Roosevelt's intentions not been significantly overturned by the successor, Truman Administration. As much of Roosevelt's intentions which were actually adopted, worked to great benefit for both the U.S.A. and western Europe, at least up through the middle of the 1960s. The question now to be addressed, against that background, is: *What are the crucially successful features of that fixed-exchange-rate system, which are fully applicable, as a matter of principle, to the vastly different world conditions of today?*

On the surface, the answer to that challenge for today, is rather elementary, and therefore readily adopted and supported by rational leading political bodies. However, as I shall indicate here, the success of such remedies requires leading roles by experts who also understand certain deeper subtleties of the matter. I explain the distinctions and their implications here.

A Basket of Commodities

In fact, the strength of the 1945-1965 Bretton Woods System, lay in the fact that the standard of value was, *in effect*, a basket of *hard commodities*. The U.S. dollar's strength as a reserve currency, was based upon the assurance that the current obligations against the U.S. dollar would be matched by the combination of an export-surplus plus gold bullion at a standard, fixed price for monetary-reserve gold. The gold-reserve system worked, because it was defended by protectionist and related regulatory measures, both internationally, and within the relevant nations themselves. It was the *physical* strength of the U.S. economy, as measurable per capita, *a strength measured in terms of rates of growth of physical productivity per capita and per square kilometer*, a strength expressed as *periods of high rate of increase in hard-commodity forms of capital formation*, which was crucial for the way in which the U.S. economy performed during the initial two decades of the post-war monetary system. This physical strength, matched with war-torn Europe's needs for both expanded volumes of U.S. agricultural products and machine-tool categories, enabled U.S. credit to stimulate a rate of growth of physical productivity, per capita, in western Europe, a growth from which Europe obtained the means to meet its obligations to the U.S.A.

In effect, in President Franklin Roosevelt's recovery policies of the 1930s, and in the 1945-1965 Bretton Woods System, the U.S.A. was carrying out the same type of economic-growth policies proposed by Dr. Lautenbach at the 1931 meeting of the Friedrich List Gesellschaft, extending credit to build up the productive powers of its customers, and thus, during 1945-1965, enriching a growing U.S. economy by providing Europe the power to repay the credit extended to it. Thus, Dr. Lautenbach's proposal had been not only congruent with the measures actually taken in the U.S.A. under President Franklin Roosevelt, a Roosevelt legacy which informed the 1945-1965 post-war economic relations between the U.S.A. and western Europe. The point to be stressed, is that the policies of both FDR and Lautenbach, were premised explicitly upon what U.S. Treasury Secretary Alexander Hamilton had defined for the U.S. Congress as the anti-Adam Smith *American System of political-economy*, the same policy represented by the leading Nineteenth-Century economists Friedrich List and Henry C. Carey, and the policies which the Friedrich List Gesellschaft represented in Germany at the time of Dr. Lautenbach's presentation of the proposed policy.

This is essentially the same view expressed by Japan and other current proponents of an ASEAN Plus Three system of cooperation in Asia. Those sectors of the international economy which have the ability to supply nations with the means to increase the latter's productive powers of labor, are to be repaid, according to appropriate medium- to long-term capital funding agreements, out of those gains in per-capita productive powers of labor, which result from the use of the relevant imported technologies.

This had been President Franklin Roosevelt's intention for post-war U.S. aid to nations and peoples he intended should be liberated from the colonialist systems and legacies of Portugal, the Netherlands, the British monarchy, and France. Roosevelt detailed infrastructure-development for Africa as an example of this policy. That policy, as it had been intended by Roosevelt, should become the basis for new forms of cooperation between those sections of the world's economy which have the ability to provide advanced technologies, and less developed regions. This policy-orientation provides the mission-orientation which a new, fixed-exchange-rate, world monetary system must adopt.

A point concerning a fixed-exchange-rate requirement, is to be emphasized, at this juncture. If the discount rate on medium- to long-term extension of international credit exceeds the levels of 1-2% per year *simple interest*, high average rates of hard-commodity capital formation are not possible generally, and, most emphatically, not possible for developing nations as entireties. If the values of relevant currencies are allowed to fluctuate under pressures from financier-oligarchical centers such as London, the general, open-market rate of borrowing-costs must rise accordingly, and must tend to be reflected, even axiomatically, in compounded interest-payment requirements, rather than merely simple interest. In effect, the very existence of a gold-standard system, such as that which London maintained world-wide, until 1931, or, a floating-exchange-rate system, such as that set into motion by President Richard Nixon's decree of August 1971, spells relatively immediate catastrophe for so-called developing nations, and ultimate ruin for the others.[3]

In the present situation, where the valuation to be placed on each and every currency of Europe and the Americas, among others, is increasingly in doubt, what constitutes the quality of durable value upon which medium- to long-term, hard-commodity capital formation could be rationally premised? In the celebrated words of Shakespeare's Hamlet: "To be, or not to be: that is the question." When it is, thus, most forcefully demonstrated, that durable forms of economic values, can not be adduced from a quantity of money, where does a measurable valuation of economic activity lie?

Enter, once again, the matter of "a basket of commodities." I mean a "basket of commodities" as that notion implicitly underlies the relative success of the 1945-1965 fixed-exchange-rate monetary system. I mean a "basket of commodities" as U.S. Treasury Secretary Alexander Hamilton's 1791 Report to the U.S. Congress **On The Subject of Manufactures** defined what became known world-wide as *The American System of political-economy*. Just as the success of the 1945-1965 trans-Atlantic system was premised upon coordinate physical-economic growth in the combined national economies of the U.S.A. and western Europe, so Hamilton, basing himself, via Vattel, on the work of Gottfried Leibniz, based the economic policies of the U.S.A. on the mutual growth of the urban industries and the rural countryside.[4] In short, sound economics premises its measurements of performance upon growth-rates, measured in physical units per capita and per square kilometer, not upon nominal (e.g., financial) prices attached to a list of produced goods.

So, in a situation in which the hard-commodity content among currencies is fluctuating, one still has the option of constructing a synthetic unit of account which is based upon an agreed basket of hard commodities. Thereafter, as currencies fluctuate, it is the currencies, not the commodities, which are given implicitly adjusted values, as based upon the basket of commodities used to define the unit. Such a synthetic unit could serve as the accounting-system of an international credit facility, as, in that sense, the basis for creating a kind of successor to SDRs.

Thus, in the matter of medium- to long-term capital

---

3. Typical of the evils fostered by a floating-exchange-rate system, is the swindle by means of which the IMF system looted so-called Latin America. The London market, which is the center of most of the world's financial speculation, would orchestrate a run against the currency of a nation of South or Central America. Then, the international monetary authorities, would intervene to require a reduction in the value of the targetted currency. Worse, they would then increase the foreign debt of the targetted nation, to compensate the international lenders for the loss in expected debt-service revenues which might otherwise be caused by the forced devaluation. *Thus, since 1971, the nations of South and Central America have, aggregately, paid vastly more debt-payment than they ever actually incurred!*

4. Today, it must be emphasized often, that the U.S. political-economy, and Constitution, echoed the influence of Gottfried Leibniz, and rejected the contrary dogma of John Locke. For example, the use of Leibniz's rebuttal of Locke: "life, liberty, and the pursuit of happiness," in the 1776 Declaration of Independence reflects this, as does Benjamin Franklin's connections to followers of Leibniz in Germany itself, such as Göttingen University's Abraham Kästner. Vattel's influence, on Hamilton and others in the Americas, is reflective of this. (See Robert Trout, "Life, Liberty, and The Pursuit of Happiness," **Fidelio**, Spring 1997.)

loans for hard-commodity investments, the relevant currencies are priced according to the basket of commodities as a standard. The loan is made in these units, not currency-prices; however, the exporter is credited with that number of synthetic units at the time the product is delivered, and repayments of the loan are determined by the price of the relevant currency, in those units, at the time that specific payment is due.

Thus, in effect, a barter-like system of medium- to long-term lending of hard commodity product, is used to approximate the "gold-reserve plus basket of commodities exported" system which operated in relevant trans-Atlantic relations during the 1945-1965 interval of a fixed-exchange-rate system.

That is the gist of the matter.

Now, examine the interim use of such a synthetic

The Lautenbach Plan for Economic Recovery

In a speech on Feb. 22, 1998, Helga Zepp-LaRouche, founder of the Schiller Institute, discussed Dr. Wilhelm Lautenbach's economic program for getting Germany out of the Depression of the 1930s. Here are excerpts.

I want to refer to the economic policy debate in Germany at the beginning of the 1930s. I do not make a comparison to the 1930s because I say that this crisis is like that of the 30s; it is quite different. But, I raise it, because it is connected to the question of what to do under conditions of a depression and a financial crisis.

Recently, in 1991, the transcript of a secret conference of the Friedrich List Society of 1931, was published. The issue was how to boost the economy under conditions of a world economic crisis. Among the participants in this conference was the president of the Reichsbank, Dr. Luther, and 30 leading economists and bankers.

And, a person who is not very well known, but deserves to be better known, Dr. Wilhelm Lautenbach, wrote a memorandum for this conference, the title of which was "The Possibilities of Boosting Economic Activities by Means of Investment and Expansion of Credit," in which he said, "The natural course for overcoming an economic and financial emergency is not to limit economic activity, but to increase it."

He pointed out that there are two different kinds of emergency situations. One, is war, earthquakes, other national catastrophes. And then there's a second type of crisis, which is economic and international, emergencies with international dimensions.

In such situations, it would be clear that more should be produced. But, if you only follow the laws of the market, this is not possible, because, in the second case, of a collapse of the financial system, you have a paradoxical situation, where, despite the fact that production already is collapsing, the demand is less than the supply. And this then leads to a tendency to decrease production even more.

If the government then adopts a program of deflation, it will tend to cut the deficit by cutting the state's expenditures, cutting prices and wages, restricting credit, and so forth and so on.

Lautenbach says that it is impossible to reduce taxes under these conditions, because the tax base is already reduced. And all such deflationary measures produce new and large losses of capital for the individual entrepreneur in commerce and industry. It makes them uncompetitive and insolvent, and it causes a reduction of production, and layoffs. It also leads to a deterioration of the banks.

Now, it is exactly this wrong approach which is presently taken by Maastricht, by the European Union, by the IMF, by the whole effort to package and solve this crisis, and not only in Southeast Asia, but in Russia, everywhere. This wrong idea.

The reduction of public expenditures is doubly counterproductive, since the public contracts and mass purchasing powers are further reduced. It leads to a collapse of production, and an increase of unemployment. And it is a downward spiral, which becomes worse and worse, and there is no bottom.

Therefore, Lautenbach says that the deflationary policy will inevitably lead to a complete economic and political catastrophe. But there is a paradox, because in a depression, you have unused productive capacities and unemployed labor. And therefore, the problem is very simple to solve: The state must inter vene, and create new national economic demand. The

Continued on next page

---

unit of trading account more closely. Examine the way in which such a unit is to be designed and managed.

It will be obvious to the reader that what is to be said on this account, involves a set of nested approximations of the exact values desired; but, that should not be considered cause for reasonable objections. The fact of the matter is, that, contrary to the *Laputa*-like superstitions which certain academic mystics spread to their credu-

lous students at Harvard and Chicago Universities and elsewhere, all prices and related set values in day-to-day economic practice, are never closer to reality, than serving as reasonable approximations; the mythical "right price" exists only in the minds of deluded persons. Contrary to utilitarians such as Jeremy Bentham, there is no asymptotic price-value upon which commodities must tend to converge in a state of "free fall." There are no random numbers in real economic processes, but only the customary charlatans who teach a dogma of random numbers.

The margin of error which may be incurred in adopting an estimated value, such as a standard basket of commodities, should be understood as a reasonable choice made, in effect, by relying upon intelligent management of the relationships by such a qualified agency, and upon an understanding rooted in good faith among the parties to the arrangement.

The Practice and the Theory

The key to establishing a reasonably determined standard unit of account for a basket of commodities, is to reject, from the outset, the reductionist input-output presumption of Britain's Piero Sraffa, for example, that consumption might be represented as a process of production of commodities by commodities. We must examine the way in which combined market-baskets of economic infrastructure (such as public works), combined with household consumption and with technologically progressive, hard-commodity forms of increasingly capital-intensive investments in capital goods of production and physical distribution, increases the relative productive powers of labor, as this is to be measured, in physical product, per capita and per square kilometer. *It is that factor of rate of growth, as expressed in hard-commodity terms, which defines the appropriate notion of assignable economic value.*

So far, so good; but, there is a catch. In some respects, such measurements of growth-rates are relatively obvious; but, therein lies an often overlooked subtlety, to ignore which may have dreadful results. Consider the more obvious kinds of measurements, and then what might appear to some to be the awfully clever subtleties.

The essential calculation to be attempted, in any rational scheme of economic studies, is what is best identified as *the potential relative population-density of the population of the national economy as a whole. The measurement to be derived from this standard, is a*

The boundary conditions that had protected the U.S. economy were obliterated by fiscal-austerity fanatic President Jimmy Carter (left) and President Richard Nixon, the ill-fated dupe of the Mont Pelerin Society.

measurement of the rate of increase, or decrease of that potential. That measurement defines what should be understood as expressing an underlying notion of economic growth. The following steps are featured.

Competent study of economic processes begins, not with the production of commodities, but, rather, the production of people. That is to say, with the development of children into becoming, decades later, functioning adult members of the economy as a whole. Indeed, here lies the natural root of the formation of capital.

To structure calculations to this effect, we must define a minimal size of a typical family household, and its included birth and mortality rates. We do this, in order to estimate what is necessary to meet the standard for growth and self-sustained well-being of that population as a whole. One defines the level of technology— e.g., a set of technologies—which allows that population to generate a corresponding net rate of physical-economic growth. We define the relationship between the adult work-force and the total population, as organized in households—that is to say, organized in the way in which viable forms of households produce the emotional and intellectual development which is to be desired in the functioning adult member of society. This establishes a rough standard for purposes of comparison.

One then defines the corresponding structural characteristics of the division of labor in the society as a whole. The first objective, is to estimate the market-baskets of household consumption, infrastructural development (e.g., public works), industrial output, and agricultural output, and to measure these, also, both per capita and per square kilometer of the total territory of the national economy. This defines sets of "market baskets" of the commodities, including professional economic services (e.g., health, education, science) required by each of these broad categories of market-baskets. These categories of consumption, plus waste, are compared with total output of the economy, as measured in the same terms. The obvious comparisons, of *better*, *less*, or *stagnant*, in rates of increase, follow.

Thus, by applying *a synthetically chosen price* to a household income measured in terms of per capita of labor-force, and also per unit of area, we have a convenient and reasonably reliable method for estimating monetary values. By adding the actual relative free energy generated by production, in addition to costs so determined, we are able to estimate both total output of the economy, and a corresponding, estimated rate of growth. *Insofar as this estimated rate of growth coincides with a corresponding rate of increase of the potential relative population-density, the estimate for rate of growth is sufficiently sound for purposes of accounting and other administrative functions respecting the economy at large.*

Notably, in a rational economy, prices are not set by anarchic free trade, but by human boundary conditions imposed upon the economic process as a whole. These

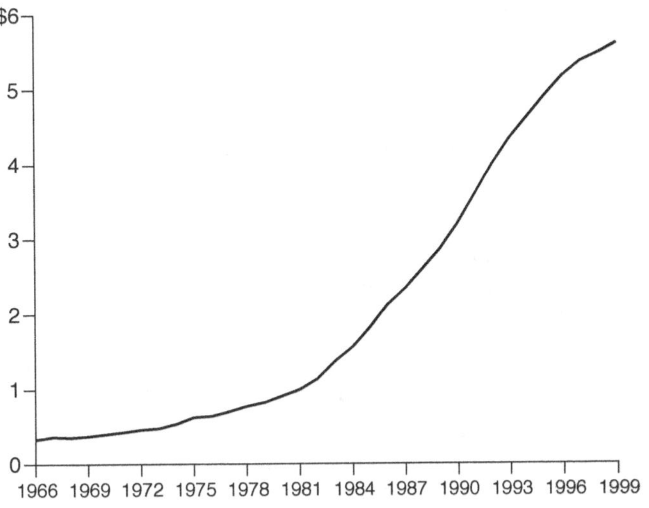

Source: U.S. Office of Management and Budget, *Budget of the United States Government, Fiscal Year 2001, Historical Tables.*

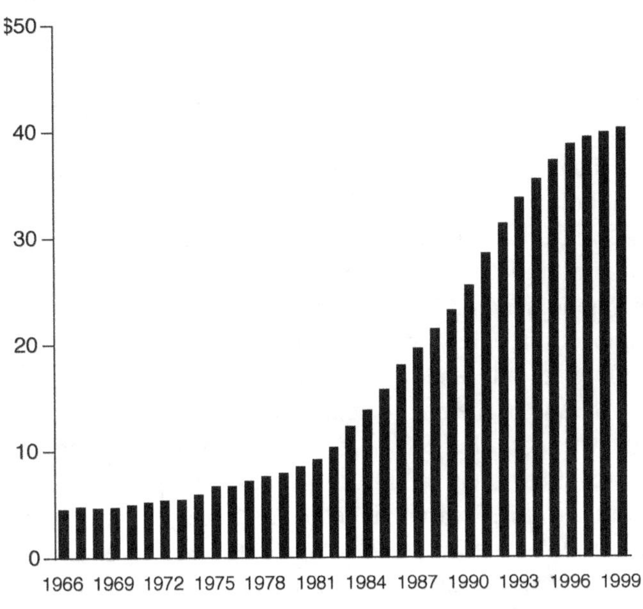

Sources: U.S. Office of Management and Budget, *Budget of the United States Government, Fiscal Year 2001, Historical Tables;* U.S. Department of Labor, Bureau of Labor Statistics, *Employment and Earnings,* June 2000.

boundaries, by their nature, must be set chiefly by governments.

Typical of such boundary conditions, are so-called "protectionist" measures, such as those former regulations of the economy which have been removed under the influence of the Mont Pelerin Society or kindred fanatics, especially since the January 1969 inauguration of the ill-fated dupe of the Mont Pelerin Society, President Richard Nixon. These protective boundaries were then assaulted, even more savagely, under the 1977-1981 reign of that free-trade and fiscal-austerity fanatic President Jimmy Carter who, with suitable historical irony, launched the chronic indebtedness of the U.S. Government which has plagued the nation since (**Figure 2**). Similarly, the decline in the percentile of national-income of the lower eighty percentile of family-income brackets, since the 1977 inauguration of President Jimmy Carter, shows a decline in the U.S. popular conditions of life, which corresponds to both the cannibalistic looting of previous improvements in productive potential, and a corresponding general lowering of the per-capita physical productivity of the labor-force as a whole.

Protectionist measures do tend to increase prices, if only in the short to medium term, as the rabid monetarists never cease in whimpering about this effect. (In the medium to long term, the higher rates of increase of productivity made possible by higher rates of hard-commodity capital formation, result in a secular decline in prices of particular products, while generally improving the quality of those products.) Thus, that increase of prices may be viewed as a rise above a so-called "free trade" level, to a "fair trade" level.

These protectionist, regulatory measures have two indispensable benefits for any economy whose government is sane enough to impose them. First, they provide direct or indirect protection to the income-levels, and therefore to the potential productivity expressed by households of operatives; this, combined with rational taxation policies, ensures that the incurred price, by government and the private sector, of maintaining the desired level of potential relative population-density, is secured. Second, in so acting, governments create the market for those medium- to long-term public and private capital investments, on which improvement in the potential relative population-density depends.

Promotion of the general welfare, which is an integral part of the fundamental constitutional law of the U.S.A.—if recently a flagrantly violated obligation—

demands that those measures which are needed to ensure the improvement of the potential relative population-density of the nation, per capita, and per square kilometer, are taken. This includes public works which no private entrepreneur could undertake as a business proposition; clear, on this account, is the responsibility of the sovereign government for the conditions of life and work of *all of the people* and of *all of the territory of the nation.*

Thus, public policy, so shaped, creates what wild-eyed dupes of the Mont Pelerin Society denounce as a willful, arbitrary intervention by the state, into the affairs of trade. Without those measures which that Society abhors, no modern economy could survive for long. Indeed, three decades-odd of that Society's ideological influence on leading governments, have created a wasteland of the once-successful economies which had grown up in the U.S. and western Europe during the 1945-1965 interval.[5] In this process, the physical-economic values which have been destroyed, since the mid-1960s, include much of the entire net development of modern infrastructure, agriculture, and industry, in Europe and the Americas, during the preceding hundred years, since the middle of the 1860s. Even two World Wars of the Twentieth Century did less net damage to Europe and the Americas than has been done by the "globalizers" and "free trade" ideologues during the recent thirty-odd years, since the ruinous first Harold Wilson Labour government came to power in the United Kingdom.

The same question may be posed in a different way. During the recent thirty-odd years, a hitherto successful form of trans-Atlantic monetary system devolved into the present stage of bankruptcy. What were the measurements which were used by policy-shapers to bring about thirty-odd years of such folly? What was so fatally wrong in the assumptions of the institutions which have been most successful, since the mid-1960s, in bringing about this magnificent, global catastrophe?

Those institutions are well-known, readily identified: they are the Mont Pelerin Society and its co-think-ers. The result which that influence has produced, does not reflect merely the accidental result of a sometimes erroneous reading of the dials by the policy-makers and managers; the catastrophe which their influence has brought about, is *systemic* in nature. It is the very design of the instruments which have been used to misguide the preponderance of the world's most influential policy-makers and managers, which has brought this epochal calamity upon the planet. It is, thus, the financial accountants and the preponderance of the economists, whose systemically aberrant standards of practice have brought this catastrophe upon us: systemically.

Granted, that the statistics lately reported and interpreted by the U.S. government and others, are, like the insane chatter about "information society" and an actually mythical "New Economy," deliberately, and increasingly falsified, that with the same intensity of desperation otherwise found commonly among those attempting, through fraudulent lures to investors and creditors, to conceal a thoroughly ripened corporate bankruptcy. However, such currently popularized frauds by governments, central bankers, and relevant others, are a symptom of the underlying problem, not the root-cause.

From this standpoint, what has failed is the empiricist system of bookkeeping, often taught under the misleading name of "economics," the system of bookkeeping which came to be associated with such names as Adam Smith, Jeremy Bentham, et al. Here, we go beyond the practical superficialities of a design of a basket of commodities, into the underlying principles, the theory, of the same matter.

The relevant theory is, in summary, as follows. I have stated these points at length, repeatedly, during the five decades since my first consolidation of my original discoveries in the field of physical economy. These need to be said again, until the students have mastered these concepts to the point of knowing the ideas, rather than merely learning the words of the description.

1. In the science of physical economy, as first defined by the relevant 1671-1716 work of Gottfried Leibniz, the specific distinction of the human species from all others, is the fact that only mankind is able to increase its species' potential relative population-density—its power— by an act of will.

   In mankind's increasing power within, and over the universe, the relevant act of will is ex-

---

5. Typical of charlatans, those U.S. and other influentials who have made a wasteland of once powerful agro-industrial economies, say that this has occurred only because the "old economy" was doomed, anyway. Like the typical charlatan, they point to the vast speculative bubble in physically worthless "New Economy" fluff, as proof that the economy which can no longer afford to pay its social welfare and infrastructural bills, is "really" a much bigger and better "new suit of clothes" for our Emperor.

pressed as the discovery of what is proven to be a universal physical principle. It is through man's accumulation of that knowledge, and man's development of the forms of cooperation through which that knowledge may be applied, that our species is permitted to choose willful changes in our species' behavior, through which our species' power in and over the universe is increased in clearly measurable forms. This measurement is expressed essentially in terms of man's increased ability to exist, per capita and per square kilometer of the territory under control of a society.

2. Insofar as the term "physical science" is used to indicate what today's classrooms accept as a notion of modern mathematical physics, both the existence of living processes and of human beings, are to be regarded as *systemically impossible mathematically*. Since the work of Clausius, Grassmann, Kelvin, Helmholtz, Maxwell, Rayleigh, and Boltzmann, among others, during the course of the Nineteenth Century, it had become conventional to say, that from the standpoint of mathematical physics so defined, the physical universe is governed by a universal law of entropy. The cause for perpetual embarrassment of the advocates of that statistical dogma was, that neither living processes, nor those processes which set mankind apart from other living processes, obey such a rule of universal entropy. Since living processes and persons are a highly efficient part of the universe, certain doubts respecting the honesty and sanity of the advocates of universal entropy had to be mentioned, even at the risk of seeming impolite, of even triggering the expectable explosion of freakishness from the pompous ass teaching the dogma to the class.

In economics, real profit of an economy as a whole, is expressed as a marginal increase of the potential relative population-density. This marginal gain corresponds to what is usefully termed the *free energy* of the system. Thus, like the living, upward evolving biosphere, the process is characteristically *anti-entropic*. In real economies, the question whether a taken profit is actually a profit to that economy as a whole, finds its answer in comparing nominal profit-rates with the actual free-energy ratio expressed in terms of correlatives of increases of the potential relative population-density. Indeed,

most of the profit attributed to the U.S. economy since August 1971, especially since January 1977, has been, in net effect, in the form of pseudo-growth: the burning-up, so to speak, of past investments in basic economic infrastructure, productive capital, and so on, as merely nominal, financial-accounting profit taken out of the real economy, rather than actual free energy added to it.

3. Therefore, chiefly in response to the popularization of the Kelvin-Clausius dogma of statistical thermodynamics, apologists for what is still considered today a conventional view of mathematical physics, adopted the term *negative entropy*, a term sometimes abbreviated as *negentropy*. According to the popularized, statistical approach to such subject-matters, the prevailing assumption is, that: a) universal negentropy does not exist; b) processes which appear, statistically, to exhibit negentropic behavior, are able to do so only by increasing the rate of entropy in the environment in which they operate. Ludwig Boltzmann's development of ideas in that direction, and the impact of Boltzmann's influence upon his students, notably Erwin Schrödinger's pathetic views on the principles of living organisms, are a notable illustration of the point.

4. Since the 1948-1952 interval, I have rejected these generally accepted mathematics classroom views on entropy and negative entropy, defining them as reflecting the influence of what is to be recognized, specifically, as the social disease of neo-Kantian Romanticism: the denial of the existence of those consciously apprehensible forms of cognitive synthesis, upon which discoveries of universal principles depend absolutely.[6] The paradoxes which show prevailing

---

6. My initial focus, from early 1948, was against the use of the term "negentropy" by Norbert Wiener. That same year, my attention broadened to include the problematical systemic features of Professor Nicholas Rashevsky's mathematical biophysics, and also that of Oparin. My views respecting the relevant systemic characteristics of living processes were, and remain in the vein of Louis Pasteur and Vladimir Vernadsky. My preference for Vernadsky's views on biogeochemistry, over the contrary view of Oparin, Rashevsky, Schrödinger, et al., does not represent the last word on Vernadsky's own development of this subject; my associate, Dr. Jonathan Tennenbaum, has been digging out, translating, and assessing some important later writings by Vernadsky on the principles of both living and cognitive processes. Notable is a September 1938 paper, whose title Tennenbaum has translated as *On the Fundamental Material-Energetic Difference Between Living and Nonliv-*

dogma on entropy/negentropy to be pathological, compel us to recognize that *the principle of life is a universal physical principle in and of itself*, in the sense that the revolutionary work of Carl Gauss's student and follower Bernhard Riemann defines the notion of a multiply-connected manifold. I have added my own original contribution to the science of physical economy, that *the principle of cognition is also a universal physical principle*. Since, as Vernadsky has presented the case for the biosphere, the anti-entropic principle of living processes, is categorically superior to non-living, statistically entropic processes, and since, as the economic history of scientific discovery shows, characteristically anti-entropic cognitive processes are superior to otherwise merely living processes, these two, respectively distinct universal physical principles, of *life* and *cognition*, must be located in their corresponding place in the body of physical science as a whole.[7]

5. At first glance, the changes in behavior which enable society to increase its potential relative population-density, are a matter of observable

---

ing Natural Bodies in the Biosphere. So far, the principal defect in these later writings by Vernadsky, is an inadequate appreciation of the relevant implications of those discoveries of Bernhard Riemann which latter contributed greatly to all of my own work on related issues of the science of physical economy. All of my relevant work of the 1948-1953 interval, was principally a reflection of my earlier refutation of I. Kant's attacks on the work of Gottfried Leibniz; hence, my recognition of the popularized notion of universal entropy as the fruit of neo-Kantian Romanticism.

7. I use anti-entropic in the same sense as I define the physical geometry of Riemann as anti-Euclidean, rather than the customary and epistemologically clumsy "non-Euclidean." Such distinctions in terminology are not merely more precise choices than the conventional ones. The lunatic effort to replace living man by devices allegedly exhibiting "artificial intelligence," has no different basis than stubborn, blind faith in defining the physical universe as fully explainable in terms of the hereditary, aprioristic, axiomatic assumptions associated with today's generally accepted, reductionist-deductive schemes of classroom mathematics. It was the Leibnizian legacy of anti-Euclidean physical geometry, as transmitted from Kästner to his student Gauss, to Riemann, which permits us to recognize that it is physics which must govern mathematics, rather than the other way around. The banning, by Riemann, of all *a priori* notions, such as those of space and time, from geometry, and the replacement of such notions by experimentally validated discoveries of universal physical principles, such as life and cognition, has been the breakthrough which opened the door to a saner understanding of the meaning of "physical universe," one in which the existence of those living cognitive beings called people, need no longer be held in doubt.

changes in the relationship between the demographically defined individual person and nature. Thus, we measure matters in terms of changes in physical values per capita and per square kilometer of surface-area. From this vantage-point, we can estimate the increase in productive powers of labor, as having the form of a change in the characteristic curvature of that Riemannian physical-space-time geometry which represents the current state of scientific and technological development of practice. In this view, the addition of a valid new universal physical principle, changes the characteristic curvature of the physical-economic domain of action. The synthesis of a validated universal physical principle, which occurs only through the sovereign, hypothesis-generating processes of individual cognition, thus becomes the form of human action, by means of which mankind's power in and over the universe is increased.

6. However, closer examination of the matter shows, that we can not limit this function of cognition to the matter of validatable discoveries of universal physical principle. Since notions of universal principle can not be transmitted solely by means of sense-perception, *the ability of society to cooperate in the selection and use of discovered physical principles, depends upon replication of the cognitive act of discovery of a principle by one mind in the mind of another.* This replication, as it occurs in circumstances such as those of Classical humanist forms of education, is known to us as a body of experimentally validated universal principles of Classical artistic forms of composition. Through those forms of art which reference the cognitive processes of mind, rather than mere sense-perception (e.g., sensual forms of pleasure and pain), we foster the forms of insight needed for effective collaboration in producing and promoting the universal physical principles upon which the anti-entropic increase of mankind's potential relative population-density depends. These Classical forms include not only what are customarily regarded as the combined plastic and non-plastic art forms, but also the development of literate forms of language, the study of history, and of other matters of statecraft, as well.

7. Thus, the manifold of such universal physical

and Classical-artistic principles represents the principled medium through which mankind acquires both the physical principles and principles of cooperation on which the increase of our species' potential relative population-density depends.

8. Three crucial points of economic policy are to be derived from the foregoing considerations. A) That the principal human source of economic growth is the education of the young, a span of development which, for the case of the most advanced economies of the mid-1960s, occupies approximately the first quarter-century of the life of increasing portions of the total population of new-born individuals. This means not only a Classical humanist form of scientific and artistic education in schools and universities, but conditions of family and community life which are emotionally and otherwise suited to the promotion of the self-development of the cognitive powers of the young individual. B) Thus, the student's reliving the re-enactment of validated original discoveries of universal physical principle, and the related role of university-centered fundamental research programs as the principal driving force for proliferation of further scientific and technological progress of the economy as a whole. C) The crucial role of the individual private entrepreneur (as distinct from the often *Golem*-like, publicly held stock corporation and holding company), especially those occupied with the kinds of machine-tool practice related to design of proof-of-principle experiments, like the comparable case of the progressive individual farmer, in pushing forward *the suitably impassioned process of technological progress*. A sane form of modern economy demands that the state create the regulated environment and basic economic infrastructure in which the function of the sovereign cognitive powers of the individual, serves as the cutting edge of technology-driven, increasingly capital-intensive forms of economic progress at large.

Thus, this form of science-technology-education-driven economic growth, is, by its nature, Riemannian in form. The addition of validated new discoveries of universal physical principles, expands the multiply-connected manifold of universal physical principles being applied. That shift in the manifold is expressed, characteristically, by a change in the implied physical-space-time curvature of action within that economy. This shift, in turn, is reflected in the anti-entropic form of increase of the potential relative population-density. It is the rate of change, the rate of increase of productivity so defined, which is the substance of the anti-entropic "free energy" ratio upon which the continued generation of true, rather than fictitious profit depends.

Those eight points summarily identify the setting within which the discussion of real rates of economic growth is to be situated.

The Global Division of Labor

As the cases of China and India underscore the point, most of the world today is imperilled by a shortage of currently usable land-area relative to large concentrations of the world's existing population. The obvious present barriers to improvement of the condition of life of the majority of the world's population, are to increase the ratio of usable to total land-area, to increase the potential population-density of those land areas, and to accelerate the effective rate of scientific and technological progress in the modes of production and household and community life.

To this end, we require the adoption of several rule-of-thumb policy agreements among nations. 1) That the number, scale, and intensity of "volcanoes" from which scientific and technological progress is erupting, must be greatly increased, and the fertility of those sites increased. 2) That, to make possible the assimilation of such scientific and technological progress, the required basic economic infrastructure (e.g., water management, power, transportation, education, health care) must be provided in all of the areas targetted for high rates of gain in productivity and living standard. 3) That the creation of long-term credit for relevant purchases of scientific and technological progress and build-up of needed infrastructure, must be greatly expanded, to enable flows from those places in which the relatively highest rates of technological progress are being generated, into the areas of greatest need and opportunity for such development of land-areas, populations, and productive economy.

This means that related policies must be crafted from the standpoint of looking approximately a quarter-century ahead. This forward span will come to be expressed in the terms of long-term credit advanced for relevant categories of capital improvements. This will represent a desperately needed new chance at life, for a shabby relic of a civilization now at the verge of destroying itself.

Such a program of global reconstruction, will echo the best features of economic cooperation between the U.S.A. and western Europe during the 1945-1965 interval. It must also represent an improved way of thinking about economy, including a sweeping, contemptuous rejection of everything associated with, or resembling the axiomatically irrationalist, *Conservative Revolution* dogma of existentialists such as Schopenhauer, Nietzsche, Martin Heidegger, Friedrich von Hayek, Ludwig von Mises, Norbert Wiener, John von Neumann, Maurice Strong, and the Mont Pelerin Society's ideologues generally. That is to say, we must think of economy in terms of physical economy, rather than placing the emphasis on nominal financial assets, and must view economy as expressing mankind's increasing power within and over the universe we inhabit. It must also express a recognition of the role of the forms of cooperation based upon the cultural principles of cognition, rather than the perverted notion of man as Hobbesian-like, of man as self-degraded into being a mere beast-like creature ruled by pleasure and pain.

There must be a new, deeper, richer conception of the notions of strategy, military and otherwise. The actual cause for warfare in the history of modern European civilization, has been nothing other than the struggle of modern oligarchies to subjugate either one another, or, more generally, to either keep populations in the condition of virtual human cattle, or, as today's Mont Pelerin ideologues do, to return mankind to such a human-cattle-like political and social condition. The insurgency of that treasonous asset of the British monarchy, the Confederacy, to destroy the U.S.A., and to ensure the perpetuation of chattel slavery, is typical of the causes for just wars, such as that led by President Abraham Lincoln, just as Europe's belated agreement to the conditions of the 1648 Treaty of Westphalia, defined the premises in international law for as much civilized life as has actually existed within extended European civilization since that time.

Today, the principal danger to civilization is from that London-centered, global financier oligarchy, which has adopted the proliferating dupes of the Mont Pelerin Society's "free trade" dogma as the instrument for destroying the existence of the sovereign nation-state, reducing the scale and life-expectancies of the majority of the human population, and degrading the survivors chiefly to the status of human cattle, of virtual Nintendo-addicted Yahoos. Those dupes, are in fact fascists, just as much as Adolf Hitler before them. If that oligarchy and its right-wing dupes, were to succeed in imposing their globalization, "free trade," and shareholder-interest ideologies, civilization would soon cease to exist on this planet for a generation or more to come. To defeat that oligarchy in that, its evil, neo-imperial enterprise, would be the only just cause for warfare among nations at this historical juncture. Otherwise, the world has no further, justifiable need of warfare, except in necessary defense of a peaceful order among sovereign nation-states.

The time has come to bring forth on this planet, the rule of man's affairs by a partnership among a community of perfectly sovereign nation-state republics, republics committed to that promotion of the general welfare which is outlined in the opening paragraphs of our 1776 Declaration of Independence, and the Preamble of our Federal Constitution. Among nations so united in a community of principle among perfectly sovereign nation-states, no justified war could occur. The principle, the general welfare of all of the people, and their posterity, of each nation, and the general welfare of each member of the community of such nations, is the only visible means by which a planet-wide state of affairs suitable for human beings can be brought into existence.

In such a community, the jewel of all civilization, is the development of the perfectly sovereign cognitive powers of the individual person. The promotion of the development of that individual, those powers, and the realization of the benefit each might contribute to present and future humanity, must be the conception which motivates all our shaping of economic policies. That must be the case in fact; that must be a shared understanding among the parties.

A basket of commodities, as I have outlined that case here, is thus to be understood as a shared commitment to do good. *The issue of economy is, therefore, not the exact price to be placed on any commodity, but the good will expressed in the way a reasonable estimate of a fair price is adopted.* On that basis, a reasonable price for a unit basket of commodities, will be the right price in practice.